Dr. Richard Knopp _____ of truth and its importance in a world dominated by relativism. If you're wondering how to communicate the truth about God in a pluralistic society that's confused about the nature of truth claims, *Truth about God* is an essential read.

— **J. Warner Wallace**, *Dateline*-featured Cold-Case Detective, Senior Fellow at the Colson Center for Christian Worldview, and author of *Cold-Case Christianity* and *Person of Interest*

Nothing is more important than knowing the *Truth About God*, and in these pages Richard Knopp powerfully addresses the questions, "What can we know?" and "How can we know it?" Don't let the small size of this book fool you; it brims with life-changing information about the God who made us and who loves us beyond belief!

— **Mark Mittelberg**, best-selling author of *Confident Faith* and *The Questions Christians Hope No One Will Ask (With Answers)*

Dr. Knopp is always brilliant and insightful, and this comes through so powerfully in *Truth About God*. This book is a guide to what faith holds on to and why. It will challenge your mind and inspire your heart to worship. *Truth About God* is a tremendous gift to help us stand strong in our battles.

— **Jud Wilhite**, Senior Pastor, Central Church (Las Vegas), and author of *Pursued*

Motivated by a practitioner's heart and informed by decades of teaching philosophy and apologetics, Richard Knopp's handy primer is an eminently useful roadmap for navigating the thorny terrain of what we can know about God. Crackling with both biblical and philosophical clarity, these pages serve to embolden and equip prospective defenders of the faith. With rigor and winsomeness, perspicacity and orthodoxy, Knopp's work, in impressively short compass, by turns resonates with the likes of Charles Taylor and John Henry Newman, C. S. Lewis and A. E. Taylor, impeccably helping fill the dire need for such substantive and streamlined treatises.

— **Dr. David Baggett**, Professor of Philosophy and Director of the Center for Moral Apologetics, Houston Baptist University

At a time when the issue of truth is being undermined and redefined, Dr. Knopp pens an excellent apologetic about truth and its foundation for all believers. It should be required reading for every leader, Gen X person, and Gen Z person in the church. He gives an extremely healthy overview of the topic and its application to our lives and ministries. Enjoy each chapter but don't over-look the rich treasure of the endnotes. A great book for a serious sermon series and for Bible studies and small group studies.

— **Dr. David Roadcup**, Professor of Discipleship at TCMI International and cofounder of e2: Effective Elders

In an age awash with slippery and sloppy notions of truth, a voice of sanity is welcome indeed. Richard Knopp is such a voice. The author covers the basics and does so well. *Truth About God* is compact but not dense, punchy yet still pithy. This is a book I will be recommending to all my students.

— **Dr. Douglas Jacoby**, apologist, author, international Bible teacher (126 nations)

Our COVID culture forced us to pivot to survive and succeed. This book will help you pivot, spiritually and theologically. They say educators make simple things profound, and communicators make profound things simple. Dr. Knopp does both. His condensing of concepts and familiarizing of phrases will better equip you to "give an account for the hope that is in you" (1 Peter 3:15, NASB) and effectively guide you to engage others with the knowable truth about the God of the universe.

In a world of ever-increasing skepticism about the very possibility of knowledge—let alone knowledge of God—Dr. Knopp presents a stout yet palatable biblical epistemology. He successfully addresses the pitfalls of both modern rationalism and postmodern subjectivism. Very concise but extremely helpful, especially for the busy life of a committed disciple.

This volume provides a concise and fresh argument for having confidence in the truth people can know about God and the gospel. It should function nicely as a primer in church settings where people want to know precisely what they can share with friends and coworkers with confidence.

TRUTH ABOUT GOD

WHAT CAN WE KNOW
AND HOW CAN
WE KNOW IT?

RICHARD A. KNOPP

RENƎW.org

Truth About God: What Can We Know and How Can We Know It?

ISBN (paperback) 978-1-949921-80-9
ISBN (Mobi) 978-1-949921-81-6
ISBN (ePub) 978-1-949921-82-3

Cover and interior design: Harrington Interactive Media (harringtoninteractive.com)

Printed in the United States of America

In gratitude for my treasured wife, Paula,
and our faith-filled children:

Nicki Green, Katie Young, and Andy Knopp

Proverbs 31:28–31

CONTENTS

GENERAL EDITORS' NOTE

We all need a thoughtful foundation for our beliefs. What makes our trust in Jesus and in the Bible sufficiently grounded? How do we know if Christianity is true? What can we know with confidence?

From the earliest days, thoughtful followers of Jesus have pointed to evidence that convinced them Jesus was who he said he was. The Gospel of Luke, for example, begins with a statement that Luke investigated the evidence and then wanted to share what he found (Luke 1:1–4). What evidence has God provided that makes faith compelling?

Richard A. Knopp is uniquely gifted to guide us in our questions. He is Professor of Philosophy and Christian Apologetics at Lincoln Christian University, where he has taught since 1983. He is the Director of Room For Doubt (www.roomfordoubt.com), a grant-funded program that seeks to encourage questions, address doubts, and strengthen Christian faith. Since 2000, he has also served as the Director of WorldView Eyes, a project that received over one million dollars from the Lilly Endowment to help high school youth understand and embrace a Christian worldview. He holds a Doctor of Philosophy in Philosophy (University of Illinois), a Master of Divinity in Theology and Philosophy (Lincoln Christian Seminary), and a Master of Arts in Philosophy (Southern Illinois University). Prior to full-time teaching, he served in two youth ministries and in a five-year preaching ministry. "Rich" and his wife, Paula, have been married since 1971, and they have three children (two daughters and a son) and seven grandchildren.

This book lays a foundation for how we can have confidence embracing Christian beliefs, such as we have listed in the Renew.org Leader's Faith Statements (see Appendix B). The book seeks to help everyday disciples live out 1 Peter 3:15: "But in your hearts revere Christ as Lord. Always be prepared to give an answer to everyone who asks you to give the reason for the hope that you have. But do this with gentleness and respect." To this end, Knopp prepares us to make a defense of our faith in well-informed and practical ways.

The following tips might help you use this book more effectively (and the other books in the *Real Life Theology* series):

1. *Questions, answers, and Scriptures.* We framed this book around two key questions. This format provides clarity, making it easier to commit crucial information to memory. This format also enables the books in the *Real Life Theology* series to support our catechism. Our catechism is a series of fixed questions and answers for instruction in church or home. In all, the series has fifty-two questions, answers, and key Scriptures. This particular book focuses on two questions that are most pertinent to knowing truth about God: "What can we know?" and "How can we know it?"

2. *Personal reflection.* At the end of each chapter are six reflection questions. Each chapter is short and intended for everyday people to read and then process. The questions help you to engage the specific teachings and, if you prefer, to journal your practical reflections.

3. *Discussion questions.* The reflection questions double as discussion-group questions. Even if you do not write down the answers, the questions can be used to stimulate group conversation.

4. *Summary videos.* You can find three- to seven-minute videos that summarize the book, as well as each chapter, at Renew.org. These short videos can function as standalone teachings. But for groups or

group leaders using the book, they can also be used to launch discussion of the reading.

May God use this book to fuel faithful and effective disciple making in your life and church.

For King Jesus,
Bobby Harrington and Daniel McCoy
General Editors, *Real Life Theology* series

INTRODUCTION

We continually ask God to fill you with the
knowledge of his will through all the wisdom
and understanding that the Spirit gives, so
that you may live a life worthy of the Lord and
please him in every way: bearing fruit in every
good work, growing in the knowledge of God.

— Colossians 1:9b–10

This book is for followers of Jesus who want to grow
in their knowledge of God and who want to help
others do the same. While this will require some mental effort, it is much more than an intellectual matter. According to Paul's prayer in Colossians 1 (quoted above), it is directly connected to who we are and how we live. I pray this book will help you grow in the

knowledge of God, have greater confidence in your own faith, and have more boldness to share your faith with others.

This short volume features material I've presented in classrooms and in hundreds of conferences, conventions, camps, and churches for over forty years. It's designed to enable you to teach yourself, but it's also designed to help you teach others. In seminary, after my major professor, James D. Strauss, explained some awesome point, he often added, "And that'll preach." He helped me see the necessity of sharing the amazing truths of God with the person in the seat at church or, in his typical words, "with the truck driver on Route 10." In that sense, I hope the material in this book "will preach"—to you and to others.

The book will stretch you, but that's what growing involves. The main text covers a lot of ground, and the extensive endnotes will prompt you to go even deeper, though they might be most helpful for preachers, teachers, and other Christian leaders who could especially benefit from additional commentary and other resources to consult.

THE BOOK WILL STRETCH YOU, BUT THAT'S WHAT GROWING INVOLVES.

The book focuses a lot on "why" questions. We started asking such questions when we were very young. Now that we are older, we know what it's like to be hammered with provoking, sometimes even exasperating, "why" questions from little ones. Apparently, everyone has a deep desire to know—and to know *why*. In that sense, everyone is a philosopher.

The book also addresses another notable philosophical question: "*How* do you know that?" I'm amazed at the sophistication of young children who ask me that question. With no formal knowledge of philosophy, they are asking a gigantic question about epistemology, which is a major branch of philosophy that studies the nature of knowledge.

Christians make all kinds of claims—claims like God created the universe; Jesus is God's unique Son who was raised from the dead; the Bible is God's Word; and the Holy Spirit guides them. But as a Christian, *how* do you know these things? This work offers some guidance on where to start with that question.

The book is divided into four chapters. Chapter 1 discusses the biblical emphasis on truth and our obligation and privilege to defend it. Chapter 2 describes some challenges to knowing truth about God that come from modernism and postmodernism. Chapter 3 explains *how* we can know truth about God. It offers important considerations about doubt and some clarifications about what it means—and doesn't mean—to know something is true. Chapter 4 attempts to demonstrate *what* truth we can know about God. It addresses the existence of

God, the character of God, the acts of God, the word of God, and the power of God.

Let's face it. If we cannot have confidence that what we say about God is true, then there's no basis or motivation for talking about the gospel (the Good News) of Jesus, making disciples, the need for holiness, the importance of the church, or Jesus' return. However, by the book's end, I hope you will develop a deeper conviction that Christianity's basic claims about God are really true.

Making a case for knowing truth about God will not be easy in the days ahead. Increasingly, our culture and even our church members are skeptical. Consider these alarming statistics:

- The percentage of Americans who believe in a "biblical view of God" fell from 73 percent in 1990 to 51 percent in 2020. Among younger Americans (ages 18–29), it fell from 64 percent to 38 percent during that 30-year period.[1]
- The percentage of atheists and agnostics in America grew from 11 percent in 2003 to 21 percent in 2018.[2]
- The youngest generation, Gen Z (ages 13–18), has twice the percentage of "atheists" (12.8 percent) compared to all previous generations (6 percent).[3]

Clearly, we have our work cut out for us! Unfortunately, Christian leaders and parents are often not adequately prepared to answer tough questions about the Christian faith, so they either give unhelpful responses or simply keep silent.[4] But for us to act effectively, we dare not be unprepared or willing to remain silent.[5]

Pursue with me Peter's appeal: "Grow in the grace and knowledge of our Lord and Savior Jesus Christ" (2 Peter 3:18). In doing so, you will, by the grace of God and the power of His Spirit, become a more mature disciple and a more effective Christian witness.

1

THE BIBLICAL EMPHASIS ON TRUTH AND ITS DEFENSE

I n his 1993 classic work *No Place for Truth*, David Wells argued that truth had become marginalized in the church.[6] And Douglas Groothuis characterized the loss of truth more generally in the title of his book *Truth Decay*.[7] Their claims are even more pertinent today, but they're not really saying anything new. Isaiah said that "truth has stumbled in the streets, honesty cannot enter. Truth is nowhere to be found" (Isaiah 59:14–15). Jeremiah declared, "This is the nation that has not obeyed the Lord its God or responded to correction. Truth has perished; it has vanished from their lips" (Jeremiah 7:28). The prophets' words are eerily applicable to our modern world.

THE IMPORTANCE OF TRUTH

THE BIBLE PLACES CONSIDERABLE emphasis on *truth*. The words "true" or "truth" appear 260 times in the New International Version. The Old Testament primarily conveys the idea of truth by the Hebrew word *emet*, which has two interrelated emphases: (1) faithfulness and (2) truth in contrast to deceit or falsehood.[8] Sometimes, especially in the Psalms, *emet* is used as the faithful quality of a *person*. God is "abounding in love and faithfulness" (Psalm 86:15), and "his faithfulness will be your shield and rampart" (Psalm 91:4c; 146:6b).

THE BIBLE PLACES CONSIDERABLE EMPHASIS ON TRUTH.

But *emet* is also used as the quality of a *statement* and its connection to reality. Joseph, when interrogating his brothers in Egypt, kept them in prison so their "words may be tested to see if [they were] telling the truth" (Genesis 42:16b).[9] The general point is that truth in the Old Testament is not just an abstract, theoretical concept; it refers to the daily witness of one's character, and it identifies statements that accurately describe reality. There is a correspondence between one's words and one's deeds, and there is a correspondence between one's words and the way the world is.[10]

The New Testament primarily refers to "truth" or to what is "true" with the Greek word *alētheia*.[11] What becomes more prominent with *alētheia* is the idea of "truth as conformity to reality in opposition to lies or errors."[12] For example, Luke records the disciples' testimony, "It is true! The Lord has risen and has appeared to Simon" (Luke 24:34). John says, "This is the disciple who testifies to these things and who wrote them down. We know that his testimony is true" (John 21:24; cf. John 19:35). Paul says in his defense, "I am not insane, most excellent Festus . . . . What I am saying is true and reasonable" (Acts 26:25).[13] And Paul affirms that God desires "all people to be saved and to come to the knowledge of the truth" (1 Timothy 2:4).

The apostle John highlights the point that truth is not merely a quality of a *proposition*; it refers ultimately to a *person*: Jesus. Jesus said, "I am the way and the truth and the life" (John 14:6). It is Jesus who is "full of grace and truth" (John 1:14; cf. 1:17). In addition, John contends that truth is not just something we *have*, it is something we *do* as well. He writes, "If we claim to have fellowship with him and yet walk in the darkness, we lie and do not live out the truth" (1 John 1:6).[14] Truth, according to John, is a way of life.

The primary point here is that the Bible says a lot about *truth*. Truth, or what is true, can apply to persons;

it can apply to propositions; and it can even apply to one's path in life.

THE IMPORTANCE OF DEFENDING TRUTH

THE BIBLE NOT ONLY speaks a lot about truth, but the Bible also provides considerable emphasis on the importance of *defending* it. The Old Testament describes numerous "champions" who fought for God's truth as opposed to a false alternative. Prominent ones include Moses opposing Pharaoh (Exodus 5–13), David facing Goliath (1 Samuel 17), Elijah challenging the false prophets of Baal (1 Kings 18), Shadrach, Meshach, and Abednego standing against Nebuchadnezzar (Daniel 3), and Daniel refusing to obey King Darius's decree (Daniel 6). The New Testament also offers notable examples of those who boldly presented and ably defended God's truth, often to their peril. Examples include John the Baptist, Jesus, Peter, Stephen, and Paul.[15]

The New Testament describes "defending" the faith with the Greek words *apologia* (a noun) and *apologeomai* (a verb). The English word "apologetics" is simply a transliteration of the Greek word, which etymologically means "reasoning from" (*apo* means "from" and *logia* refers to "reason/logic"). This reveals that the core nature of the Christian defense of truth is based on *reason*, not on emotion. It also shows that the use of reason in defending God's truth is a *biblical* practice and imperative, not just a modern concept.[16]

New Testament examples illustrate this. Peter says, "Always be prepared to give an answer [*apologia*] to everyone who asks you to give the reason [*logos*] for the hope that you have" (1 Peter 3:15). And Paul repeatedly makes his "defense" to charges against him.[17] He even claims that he was "put here for the defense [*apologia*] of the gospel" (Philippians 1:16). Another verb form of the idea is *dialegomai*, which is frequently used to describe Paul's reasoning with non-Christians.[18]

A primary takeaway here is that the Bible, and more specifically the New Testament, notably stresses that the *truth* about God stands in contrast to false alternatives; this truth was, and should be, *defended*; and it can be, and should be, defended with *reason*. It is no wonder, then, that New Testament preaching underscores that the resurrection of Jesus was accompanied by "many convincing proofs" (Acts 1:3); all Israel can be "assured" that God made Jesus both Lord and Messiah" (Acts 2:36); and God has "given proof" of his coming judgment by raising Jesus from the dead (Acts 17:31).

> THE CHRISTIAN DEFENSE OF TRUTH IS BASED ON REASON, NOT ON EMOTION.

Given the condition of our culture and many churches, I am convinced that Christian apologetics—defending God's truth—is needed now more than ever before. But we need to be adequately prepared. So let's see what we can learn about knowing truth about God and being better able to defend it.

REFLECTION & DISCUSSION QUESTIONS

1. Do the statistics presented in the book's introduction alarm you? Which ones? Why do you think that doubts and skepticism about God and Christianity seem to be increasing?

_____

_____

_____

_____

2. In our culture, people often question and criticize the notion of absolute truth—the notion that there can be "truth for everyone." What examples of such questions or criticisms can you describe? Do you think this perspective is also present in the church?

_____

_____

_____

_____

_____

3. The chapter discussed Old Testament and New Testament perspectives on truth. Identify one or two characteristics of truth that seem especially important. Explain why.

_____

_____

_____

_____

_____

4. The chapter claimed that, according to Scripture, truth is not just something we have, it is something we do as well. What do you think it means for someone to "live out the truth" (1 John 1:6)?

_____

_____

_____

_____

_____

5. If someone asked you to give a defense for the hope you have in Jesus (1 Peter 3:15), what are some responses you would give?

_____

_____

_____

_____

_____

_____

6. How confident do you feel defending your faith by giving good reasons for it? On a 1–10 scale (with 10 being extremely confident), where would you place yourself? What steps can you take to increase your level of confidence?

_____

_____

_____

_____

_____

_____

2

CHALLENGES TO KNOWING TRUTH ABOUT GOD

W hy do so many people deny we can know truth about God? There are many reasons, but a main one is that our Western culture is permeated with the consequences of several hundred years of philosophy that have created this skepticism. Philosophically, two major rivers flow into the cultural ocean in which we now swim: *modernism* and *postmodernism*. The bottom line is that modernism and postmodernism, while they exhibit notable disagreements with each other, actually *join forces to repudiate the possibility of knowing truth about God*. It's a kind of double whammy for the Christian.

This chapter will focus on the *philosophy* of modernism and the *philosophy* of postmodernism. However, there is a *cultural* sense according to which we can think of a modern culture and a postmodern culture. This *cultural* sense pertains more to social values, economic systems, and communication techniques.[19] One reason why it's important to distinguish between the cultural and philosophical senses is that some Christians unknowingly advocate postmodernism—the philosophy—when they are really thinking about postmodern *culture*. I contend that most people undeniably live in a postmodern *culture*, but this does not mean that we should endorse postmodernism as a *philosophy*.[20] As this chapter indicates, both philosophical modernism and philosophical postmodernism pose a serious threat to the truth claims of Christianity.

THE CHALLENGE OF MODERNISM

THE PHILOSOPHY OF MODERNISM received its impetus during the Enlightenment—a period that includes René Descartes (1596–1650), David Hume (1711–1776), and Immanuel Kant (1724–1804). In general, the Enlightenment stressed that humans should be freed from the superstitions and authority of religion and construct a society based on reason, empirical evidence, and scientific discovery.[21] Even though Descartes and Kant believed in God, all three of these philosophers helped dismantle our capacity to know truth about God.

René Descartes coined a famous phrase: "I think; therefore I am."[22] He used reason and turned inward to the self. He was trying to give an absolutely certain foundation for knowledge, and he believed his own existence provided that certainty. After all, it seemed impossible to doubt his own existence. However, since Descartes based knowledge within himself, it seemed he could only be certain of the ideas *in his own mind*. For many critics of Descartes, it wasn't clear that he could really know anything outside his own mind. So, ironically, Descartes's pursuit of certainty ended up laying the groundwork for skepticism. Though Descartes gave an argument for God's existence, his method actually diminished, if not destroyed, knowing truth about God.[23]

David Hume was a strong empiricist. He believed that everything we know, or can know, must come only from sense experience—from the physical senses. In his view, this excludes the possibility that we can know anything in the realm of metaphysics (what is beyond the world of sense experience). Any metaphysical claims—including claims about God—deserve only to be burned, because they are unknowable folly.[24] Hume's skepticism denies we can know *anything* about God. And Hume continues to have enormous influence in university classrooms and in our culture today.

Immanuel Kant believed in God, but like Hume he also denied we can have any *metaphysical* knowledge, which means we cannot know anything about God. Kant was actually trying to salvage belief in God, but he limited all of our knowledge and put God beyond its range. He summarized it this way: "I therefore found it necessary to deny *knowledge* [of metaphysics and God] in order to make room for *faith*."[25] He believed that many attacks against God were due to philosophers using their reason to speculate about metaphysical notions. By showing that reason cannot legitimately extend into the realm of metaphysics, he could undermine their baseless, atheistic attacks. But this had a disastrous consequence: we can believe in God; we just cannot know anything about him. As theologian Kirk MacGregor puts it, "From Kant's perspective . . . there may be a God, but there is nothing we can really say about him as to his being an object of our knowledge."[26]

THE CHALLENGE OF POSTMODERNISM

POSTMODERNISM AS A PHILOSOPHY denies that anyone can objectively know the world around us as it really is. We only see the world with different lenses (e.g., with different languages, races, genders, ages, personal experiences), and we project these cultural or personal notions onto the world.[27] As a result, there is no single reality for everyone; there are only multiple realities constructed by different groups or individuals, often fighting for power to dominate others.

In one sense, the philosophy of postmodernism is a *rejection* of key principles of modernism (see Table 1: Modernism vs. Postmodernism).[28] In another sense, postmodernism is an *extension* of modernism by playing out the consistent implications of modernism. Modernism uses reason to be skeptical of religious authority and metaphysical knowledge, but postmodernism applies skepticism to *everything*, including to reason itself.[29]

MODERNISM	POSTMODERNISM
Absolute truth is discoverable.	There is no universal or absolute truth.
We can have certainty based on a solid foundation of facts.	We have only skepticism.
All humans have the same rationality.	Different individuals and groups have different rationalities.
We know things objectively.	Objective knowledge is not possible, because we always see with the bias of our own perspective.
Reason and science reign and are often used to reject religion.	We should be skeptical of everything, including reason and even science.

Table 1

THE LOSS OF TRUTH ABOUT GOD

WHILE BOTH MODERNISM AND postmodernism offer something valuable to the Christian faith,[30] in their stronger and more secular forms, they pose a serious challenge to our knowledge of God and to biblical Christianity. Both deny we can have knowledge of God.[31] And this is the sentiment of many in our communities (if not also our churches), even if they don't know much, if anything, about Descartes, Hume, Kant, or later philosophers.

One form of modernism today is illustrated by secular humanism and by the so-called "new atheists," such as Richard Dawkins, Sam Harris, and Lawrence Krause, who have enormous influence through their popular books and online presence. They use science to attack religion—and Christianity in particular.[32] A notable postmodernist example is Jean-Francois Lyotard who emphasizes we must have an "incredulity toward metanarratives."[33] This means there is no story that is true for *everyone*. There is no metanarrative that rises above all other stories or narratives. As a consequence, it is not possible to have a gospel that can rightly claim to be true for the whole world. The Great Commission of Jesus (Matthew 28:18–20) is completely undermined. So whether it's from modernism or postmodernism, truth about God is threatened.

One point to keep in mind is that many deny knowledge of a God *constructed by philosophers*, but not necessarily the God *portrayed in Scripture.* As Alasdair MacIntyre explains, "The God in whom the nineteenth and twentieth centuries came to disbelieve had been invented only in the seventeenth century."[34] We might put it this way: The God that many *reject* is often the unbiblical God they *project.* A practical application of this would be to ask someone about the God they reject. Wait for the response. Then you can likely say, "I don't believe in that God either."

The God presented in the Bible is not a philosopher's abstract God; he is a personal God who creates, reveals himself, and comes to us. The philosopher's God is illustrated by Thomas Paine, a notable eighteenth-century deist who claimed God is knowable by reason in creation, but only in creation. Reason alone can determine that God is a "first cause," the cause of all things.[35] But Paine's God is merely a distant God. His God is not a miracle-working God. His God has not come in the flesh to save us. His God is not the God of the Bible.

> THE GOD THAT MANY REJECT IS OFTEN THE UNBIBLICAL GOD THEY PROJECT.

As we proceed to think about knowing truth about God, we want to make sure the God we can know from sources *outside of* Scripture (like from nature and reason) is the God who is also revealed *within* Scripture.

REFLECTION & DISCUSSION QUESTIONS

1. Have you been exposed to the terminology and ideas of modernism and postmodernism before reading this chapter? If not, what were your first impressions? If you have, how has this chapter confirmed or changed your views?

_____

_____

_____

_____

_____

2. Using Table 1 as a starting point, define modernism and postmodernism in your own words.

_____

_____

_____

_____

_____

3. Which of these perspectives—modernism or postmodernism—has had more of a direct impact on you and on those around you? Give examples.

_____

_____

_____

_____

_____

4. One underlying point of this chapter is that for many, faith is completely separated from reason and knowledge. The sentiment is, "Just believe; reasons and evidence are either inadequate or irrelevant." Do you see any examples of this view in your culture or even among some Christians? Explain.

_____

_____

_____

_____

_____

5. In your experience, why do people reject God or why are they skeptical about God? Are some of the reasons more than just intellectual in nature? What other factors might be involved?

_____

_____

_____

_____

_____

6. Many people reject a god who is very different from the God described in Scripture. Based on this chapter and your own experiences, describe some unbiblical perceptions of God you've encountered. Also, discuss how you can better describe the God presented in the Bible.

_____

_____

_____

_____

_____

_____

3

HOW CAN WE KNOW TRUTH ABOUT GOD?

Answer: We can know truth about God through God's general revelation in creation and special revelation in Scripture, in Jesus the Savior, and in the impact of the Holy Spirit.

For since the creation of the world God's invisible qualities—his eternal power and divine nature—have been clearly seen, being understood from what has been made, so that people are without excuse.
— Romans 1:20

---

laiming to know truth about God forces us to consider two giant philosophical questions: *What is truth?* and *What is knowledge?* These are questions about "epistemology," a major area of philosophy that means a "study of knowledge."[36] In this chapter, I will offer some highlights on the nature of truth and knowledge, and then draw some applications to knowing truth about God that include practical considerations about doubt.

WHAT IS TRUTH?

PILATE POSED THIS QUESTION to Jesus in John 18: *What is truth?* Jesus offered no philosophical answer. However, he did say he came into the world "to testify to the truth" and that "everyone on the side of truth listens to me" (John 18:37c). When we address this question from a philosophical perspective, three main theories are offered on the nature of truth: (1) the correspondence theory, (2) the coherence theory, and (3) the pragmatic theory. According to the correspondence theory, a statement is true if it *corresponds* to the way the world is.[37] According to the coherence theory, a statement is true if it *coheres* with—or fits with—other statements we take to be true. According to the pragmatic theory, a statement is true if it *works*.[38] Each of these philosophical theories provides legitimate insights into the nature of truth, and the Bible incorporates some facet of each one.

Some version of the *correspondence* theory is foundational to the biblical notion of truth.[39] When the disciples said, "It is true! The Lord has risen" (Luke 24:34), they were claiming that the statement "the Lord has risen" corresponds to reality.[40] It was an *objective* truth claim. In other words, the truth of the statement is not determined by how we feel about it or whether we agree with it, but by whether it describes what actually occurred.

The *coherence* theory rightly emphasizes that what we regard as true often depends on other truths we accept. One application is that underlying worldview beliefs can heavily influence what one will accept as true. For example, if one's worldview rejects God's existence, then the statement "God has raised this Jesus to life" (Acts 2:32) will likely be rejected. On the other hand, if one's worldview accepts God's existence, then the truth of other statements (for example, about Jesus' resurrection or God's revelation) will likely be accepted as true—because they cohere or consistently fit with one another.

The *pragmatic* theory highlights a prominent sentiment in our "post-truth" culture:[41] Truth is not so much about objective facts but about what accomplishes our agenda.[42] We just want what works. *That* is what is true. We see it in politics, in social media, in family and church communication, and even in "scientific" claims. The valued commodity is *power*, not principle.[43] In response to this idea, while the Bible talks about how the Christian faith "works" (for example, it should produce good fruit),[44] this is very different from adopting a pragmatic theory of truth, which claims that something is true simply because it works. Against this view, we should see that the Christian faith works *because it is true;* it is not to be considered true simply *because it works.*

Even with these qualifications, I suggest that knowing truth about God includes insights from all three of these perspectives on truth. What we accept as true should *correspond* to reality; it should *cohere* with the vast array of rational, empirical, and existential considerations we regard as true; and it should generate valuable *pragmatic benefits* that are intellectual, social, psychological, emotional, and spiritual.

WHAT IS KNOWLEDGE?

To CLAIM WE KNOW truth about God requires some understanding of what we mean by "knowledge." What is knowledge? Everyone claims to know all kinds of things. I know I'm typing right now. I know I was born in Corinth, Kentucky. I know 9 times 9 equals 81. I know how to edit videos in Final Cut Pro. I know my wife, Paula. I know I have a headache. Clearly, we use the word "know" in many different ways, and we have different means by which we think we know something. Some of these knowledge claims are supported by personal experience, some by historical records, some by memory, and some more directly by our mind or reason.

While philosophers vigorously debate various views, the basic formula to describe knowledge was classically characterized by Plato as "justified true belief."[45] If we genuinely know something, it seems necessary that we also believe it. (It's hard to see how one can rightly claim to know cows give milk but not believe it.) But it's possible to believe something that is false. So to know something seems to require that it also be *true*.[46]

But how do we know anything is true? The basic answer is that we must have some *justification* or warrant for thinking it is true. It's not enough just to have true belief in order to have genuine knowledge. For example, I might have a true belief that I have ten coins in my pocket, but it might just be a lucky guess. Plato would say this is just "true opinion," not knowledge.[47] I think you would agree.

GUIDING PRINCIPLES ON KNOWLEDGE AND DOUBT: CERTAINTY VS. CERTITUDE

How CERTAIN CAN WE be in what we claim to "know"? I know for certain that I'm drinking coffee now. But what about the premise of the movie *The Matrix*—that everything is just an illusion?[48] While this seems pretty ridiculous, I'm forced to admit I cannot know *with absolute certainty* that it's not some illusion. This prompts a couple of important points: (1) If "knowing truth" requires that I be absolutely certain about it without any possibility of being mistaken, then I do not know the truth about much of anything! (2) If I can't be absolutely intellectually certain, then some level of doubt seems inevitable.

These two points are especially relevant to Christians. First, many Christians think having any doubts about God is dangerous and should be disapproved.[49] Second, some Christians, especially younger ones, rightly understand that having at least periodic doubts about God is inescapable, because they cannot be absolutely certain about God. One unfortunate consequence is that those with doubts might simply not express those doubts to anyone who might be able to help. And when they do express their doubts, they too often receive only "trite and unhelpful answers."[50]

Given this problematic situation, here are some guiding principles we should understand and clearly communicate to Christians and non-Christians—to adults and to youth alike.

1. *Having genuine knowledge about something does not require that we be absolutely certain it's true.*[51]

2. *We cannot be absolutely certain in an intellectual sense that our truth claims about God are true.* We cannot provide "proof" in the sense that it's inconceivable for a reasonable person to doubt it.[52] However, it is still possible for us to have genuine knowledge about God if we can have sufficient justification for our truth claims about God.

3. *Lacking absolute certainty or proof, especially about metaphysical claims, is not a unique condition for Christians.* No one has that kind of certainty or proof. If we mean by "proof" something that is "beyond any possible doubt," then God's existence cannot be proven. But as Christian philosopher Stephen Evans contends, "Proof in this sense is an unrealistic ideal for both the theist and the atheist."[53]

4. *Having some doubts about God may be intellectually inevitable and therefore understandable.* So we should not categorically condemn those who experience some doubts about God. And Christians should also avoid making claims about having a level of certainty that is not attainable.[54] Austin Fischer poignantly observes,

> I've always found that unbelievers are much less offended by the hypocrisy of our morality than they are the hypocrisy of our certainty. . . . What unbelievers fail to understand is how we

[Christians] can pretend to be certain of things we obviously cannot be certain of.[55]

In other words, we need to be more humble and avoid any appearance of arrogance.

5. *Doubt is not the same as disbelief.* I believe a strong case can be made that the apparent condemnations of doubt in the New Testament (for example, Matthew 14:31; 21:21; James 1:6), are referring to doubt *as disbelief,* not to doubt *as lacking absolute intellectual certainty.*[56] The father of the possessed boy illustrates the difference. He exclaimed to Jesus, "I do believe; help me overcome my unbelief" (Mark 9:24b). This exemplifies how it's possible to believe something strongly yet still have doubts about it. He strongly believed, but he did not have absolute certainty. In that sense, he had *doubt* but not *disbelief.*[57]

IT'S POSSIBLE TO BELIEVE SOMETHING STRONGLY YET STILL HAVE DOUBTS ABOUT IT.

6. *It is helpful to distinguish between having intellectual certainty and having a comprehensive certitude.* While we cannot have absolute intellectual certainty in knowing truth about God (for example, using arguments and evidence from nature or history), I propose we can have "certitude" (a sufficiently

justified conviction) in knowing truth about God. This consists of an *inner assurance* that uses, but goes beyond, mere intellectual argument or external evidence. (In the next chapter, I will discuss how this certitude incorporates the internal witness of the Holy Spirit.)

The New Testament talks about "proof" and "certainty." For instance, Luke says Jesus "gave many *convincing proofs* that he was alive" after his crucifixion (Acts 1:3).[58] However, such passages should not be taken in the sense of providing *absolute intellectual certainty.* Matthew even acknowledges that some of those who saw the resurrected Jesus still "doubted" (Matthew 28:17). Instead, the *certitude* (or justified conviction) we can possess about God is consistent with the nature of Christian faith. Faith is the "confidence" (NIV) or the "assurance" (NASB) in what is hoped for; yet it is still "about what we do not see" (Hebrews 11:1).

These six guiding principles should greatly encourage those who face instances of doubt. Some doubts may be inevitable because we do not have absolute intellectual certainty. As a result, we should not only allow doubts; we should encourage their expression.[59] The good news is that our doubts can be adequately addressed.

So how can we know truth about God in the sense of having *certitude*—a justified inner conviction that includes many different considerations? How can we attain genuine knowledge of anything, but more specifically, of God?

THE SOURCES OF TRUTH AND KNOWLEDGE

GENERALLY SPEAKING, WE CAN identify four sources for knowledge of anything: (1) reason, (2) sense experience, (3) inner experience, and (4) information from others. These four sources significantly overlap and interact, but together they offer a common-sense way to distinguish how we can know truth about anything. More specifically, I propose we can know truth *about God* from these same four sources.

1. *Using Reason to Know Truth About God.* Our minds have amazing power, and God has endowed us with the capacity, and the responsibility, of utilizing reason in proper and effective ways. We are to "reason together, says the LORD" (Isaiah 1:18, ESV) and provide a reasoned answer (*apologia*) for the hope we have in Christ (1 Peter 3:15).

However, an important qualification needs to be registered about reason. Human reason can be used improperly, as though it is an *autonomous, purely human* instrument that is completely separated from God. Paul talks about how the thinking of those who do not acknowledge God can become "futile" (Romans 1:21) because they exchange "the truth about God for a lie" (Romans 1:25). Those who are "separated from the life of God" live "in the futility of their thinking" and "are darkened in their understanding" (Ephesians 4:17–18).

However, using reason to know truth about God does not mean we are necessarily using reason *autonomously*; nor does it mean we are "rationalists."[60] Reason is not autonomous.[61] It cannot, and should not, replace faith. Instead, reason should be seen as having an *adequate but limited capacity* to discover truth about God.

2. *Using Empirical Experience to Know Truth About God.* Another way we can know truth, including truth about God, is from empirical experience—experience that comes through our physical senses. We see, hear, touch, taste, and smell. Empirical experience gives us knowledge of physical reality.[62]

Initially, it might seem no one can have any empirical knowledge of God, because God is "spirit" (John 4:24).[63] While this seems true for religions like Hinduism, Buddhism, and some approaches to Christian theology, it is not true for the biblical characterization of God.[64] Biblical Christianity offers a God who is not merely some indetectable Spirit. Scripture stresses that God acts in nature and in history. So we can know some things about the non-empirical Spirit-God by observing the empirical *effects* of God's acts.[65]

Empirical knowledge of God can be inferred through *natural revelation*—"from what has been made" (Romans 1:20). Indeed, "The heavens declare the glory of God; the skies proclaim the work of his hands" (Psalm 19:1). This means some knowledge of God can be gleaned from nature itself—from the macro-world of cosmology to the micro-world of cells and DNA.

In addition, the ultimate empirical expression of God is Jesus Christ. He was the "Word" who was "with God" and who "was God" (John 1:1) and who "became flesh and made his dwelling among us" (John 1:14). As a result, many in first-century Palestine saw, heard, and touched him (1 John 1:1–3).[66] This was one way they learned truth about God. By extension, we can too.

3. *Using Inner Experience to Know Truth About God.* Of course, empirical experience (using our five senses) generates an *inner* awareness. When we see an oak tree, the sense experience of an "outer" world becomes an "inner" experience. And using our reason is also an "inner" experience. So with these considerations, there is not a sharp distinction between reason, empirical experience, and inner experience. However, what I mean here by "inner experience" points more to our deepest feelings as well as to our conscience. It highlights our "existential" awareness: Who am I? What value, if any,

do I have? Is there any ultimate meaning to my life? Such questions are not just a matter of what we *think* about ourselves; they focus on how we *feel* deeply within ourselves.

Inner experience is typically regarded as a *subjective* experience—an experience that arises *from within oneself*. As such, it can be greatly unreliable. Your inner experience may conflict with my inner experience. And your emotions, feelings, and even your conscience can change from day to day. If all we have is our personal, subjective experience, we would have no basis for rationally resolving our notable disagreements: "I feel this way; you feel that way. Let's fight about it!"

As a result, it's important to emphasize *objective* truth rather than *subjective* truth. *Objective truth* is true regardless of how one feels about it or even whether one accepts it.[67] The basic claims of Christianity are *objective* truth claims, and we should not exclusively or even primarily rely on inner experience to give truth about God. However, it's still important to note that Scripture itself affirms the value of inner experience.[68] In what follows, we'll consider two sources of truth about God from inner experience: the conscience and our deepest desires or needs.

- *Our Conscience.* One of the elements of inner experience is the conscience. The conscience certainly involves the use of reason, but conscience cuts deeper than mere rational contemplation. Conscience impacts the will and interacts with our emotions. All humans seem to possess the faculty of conscience that points toward moral truth, which is ultimately justified by God as the source of moral law.

However, while the conscience *can be* a source of truth, it can also be "corrupted" (Titus 1:15) and "seared as with a hot iron" (1 Timothy 4:2). That is, it can be desensitized. Even so, the conscience connects everyone with core principles about what is most fundamentally morally right or wrong. Paul affirms that even the Gentiles— those "who do not have the law"—still "do by nature things required by the law"; they "show that the requirements of the law are written on their hearts, their consciences also bearing witness" (Romans 2:14–15a). The conscience may not speak with specific words, but as John Frame describes it, "What it lacks in verbal precision, it gains in intimacy."[69] The conscience can be a powerful source that offers an internal witness to truth that is grounded in God. Jesus also seems to suggest the Holy Spirit works in conjunction with our

SCRIPTURE ITSELF AFFIRMS THE VALUE OF INNER EXPERIENCE.

conscience to bring moral and spiritual conviction.[70]

- *Our Deepest Desires or Needs.* A second source of truth that comes from inner experience is *our deepest desires or needs* for such things as meaning, love, and forgiveness.[71] At one level, everyone experiences meaning, love, and forgiveness. They find meaning from jobs, achievements, hobbies, etcetera, and they have relationships of love and forgiveness. But I am referring to an *ultimate* kind of meaning, love, and forgiveness—a kind that is not merely "constructed" but one that is "discovered."[72] This kind of meaning points to something (or someone) *beyond* us that is not fully explainable as merely arising *within* us. They are desires and needs that, as C. S. Lewis notes, are never fully satisfied in *this* life.[73]

In some ways, these deep existential desires or needs may actually point to divine truth more powerfully than mere intellectual contentions. The psalmist laments, "How long must I wrestle with my thoughts and day after day have sorrow in my heart?" (Psalm 13:2a); yet he rejoices in God's salvation (Psalm 13:5). Jesus exhorts the "weary and burdened" to come to him, so he can give "rest" to their "souls" (Matthew 11:28–29). Paul confesses how "wretched" he is (Romans 7:24);

yet he rejoices because his need for deliverance is satisfied through Christ, and he now has "no condemnation" (Romans 7:25; 8:1). These are examples that go beyond objective evidence; they spotlight deep human needs that demand a truth—a truth about God—that adequately satisfies them.

4. *Using Information from Others to Know Truth About God.* Much of what we know is not personally and directly acquired—by reason, by physical sense, or by inner experience. Instead, we learn from others: we read, we watch, and we listen. As a result, a primary source of much of what we know comes from others. In this section, I highlight two sources of knowledge that come from persons outside ourselves: *special revelation* and *tradition.*

• *Special Revelation as a Source of Truth About God.* Whereas *natural revelation* is a source of truth available to everyone, *special revelation* comes from God and is given to specific people in specific times and circumstances. God "speaks." The writer of Hebrews summarizes it: "In the past God spoke to our ancestors through the prophets at many times and in various ways, but in these last days he has spoken to us by his Son" (Hebrews 1:1–2a).[74]

Special revelation has been communicated in various ways (e.g., dreams, visions, a burning bush). But as this verse in Hebrews says, God's special revelation eventually and ultimately came to us "by his Son."

In addition, some of what was revealed was *written* and was incorporated in Christian Scripture, which provides a source of truth about God. It reveals what would otherwise be a "mystery."[75] Of course, other religions have their own scriptures, and the Bible itself explicitly warns against "false prophets."[76] So any specific claims to truth will need to be critically examined and compared. But if the Christian Scriptures can be sufficiently validated, especially when compared with its religious rivals, then we can be confident that it offers an indispensable source for knowing truth about God.

- *Tradition as a Source of Truth About God.* Compared to many Protestant groups, tradition has not typically been valued as much by the Restoration Movement, with which I have been closely affiliated. Alexander Campbell, one of the Restoration Movement's pioneers, and the movement in general have strongly resisted church tradition as authoritative, especially as expressed in various creeds.[77] Our movement has been known as "non-creedal": "No creed but Christ!" has been one motto.

In response, I want to stress that we should never elevate church tradition or creeds to the same level of authority as Scripture.[78] Jesus himself condemned the Pharisees because they "nullify the word of God for the sake of [their] tradition" (Matthew 15:6). And unfortunately, I suspect some denominations and local churches have occasionally wielded tradition with near-biblical authority. However, *I suggest that the insights of Christian leaders throughout history can be an important and informative source of truth about God.* As preeminent as Scripture should be, we can also learn truth about God from others throughout Christian history who were deeply devoted to Christ.[79]

In this chapter, I addressed the basic question, "How can we know truth about God?" In response, I identified four basic sources of knowing truth about anything, including God: reason, empirical experience, inner experience, and information from others.[80] Properly understood and applied, these four sources offer a valuable framework for knowing truth about God. The next chapter considers another critical question, "What truth can we know about God?"

REFLECTION & DISCUSSION QUESTIONS

1. What personal experiences have you had with doubting God or his truth? What do you know about the experiences of others?

_____

_____

_____

_____

_____

2. Review the six guiding principles when it comes to doubt. Which one is most challenging to you? Which is most helpful? Why?

_____

_____

_____

_____

_____

_____

3. This chapter discusses four primary sources of truth and knowledge: reason, empirical experience, inner experience, and information from others. Which have you relied upon the most in your faith journey?

_____

_____

_____

_____

_____

4. Is all doubt bad? Is any doubt okay? What kind(s) of doubt might be okay? (Suggestion: Visit roomfordoubt.com and access more resources on doubt.)

_____

_____

_____

_____

_____

_____

5. How has tradition played a role in forming or
   defining your beliefs about God?

   _____

   _____

   _____

   _____

   _____

   _____

   _____

6. How can you use the information in this chapter to
   help someone as they struggle with doubt?

   _____

   _____

   _____

   _____

   _____

   _____

   _____

4

WHAT TRUTH CAN WE KNOW ABOUT GOD?

Answer: We can know truth about God's existence, character, actions, word, and power.

Praise him for his acts of power; praise
him for his surpassing greatness.
— Psalm 150:2

In the previous chapters I emphasized the prominence of truth and its defense in the Bible; I presented some challenges to knowing truth about God; and I laid some philosophical and theological foundations for knowing truth about God, including the point that knowing truth about God does not require that we have intellectual certainty. Instead, I proposed we can have *certitude*, a justified conviction based on a wide variety of considerations. In this chapter, I examine some of those considerations and contend we can know truth about the *existence* of God, the *character* of God, the *actions* of God, the *word* of God, and the *power* of God.

THE EXISTENCE OF GOD

MANY IN OUR WORLD do not accept the existence of any God (atheists), and many do not think we can know whether or not God exists (agnostics).[81] For atheists and agnostics, being able to know God exists is not possible. In spite of their sentiment, I'm convinced a strong case can be made for knowing God exists—the kind of God portrayed in Scripture.

Various arguments for God's existence have been offered that are based on *natural* revelation—what is given in nature. Some see these as "proofs," but I have explained that "proving" God in the sense of producing absolute intellectual certainty without any possibility of doubt is unreasonable, because it's unachievable. As a result, it's better to construe such arguments as "pointers" rather than "proofs."[82] Pointers in nature are powerful, but they are not adequate in themselves to reveal the God of the Bible. We also need *special* revelation.[83] However, these pointers from natural revelation can provide a compelling case that justifies our claim to know of God's existence. In this section, I highlight two pointers to God's existence: the existence of the universe and the design of the universe.

1. *The Existence of the Universe Points to God.* One approach, called the *cosmological* argument, examines the very existence of the universe as a pointer to God.[84] The big question is this: How can we explain the existence of the universe? Two logical options exist: (1) the universe has *always* existed or (2) the universe *came into* existence. Both Aristotle the philosopher (385–322 BC) and Thomas Aquinas the Christian theologian (1225–1274) argued that, even if the universe is *eternal*, God's existence is still necessary.[85] However, in the twentieth century, science provided a strong case that the universe is *not eternal*—that it had a beginning.

The scientific case that the universe came into existence prompted the Christian philosopher William Lane Craig to highlight a particular version of the cosmological argument called the *Kalam* argument.[86] The structure of the argument is quite simple:

> Premise 1: Whatever begins to exist has a cause.
>
> Premise 2: The universe began to exist.
>
> Therefore, the universe has a cause.[87]

The truth of premise one is rooted in a deep intuition as well as universal experience that things that come into existence cannot cause their own existence. In other words, something cannot come from nothing. The adage, "You can't get blood from a turnip," makes a similar point, but in this case, there is at least *something*: the turnip! On the other hand, if the physical universe *came into* existence, then there was a prior condition in which there was truly *nothing*. And something—whether it's the universe or any physical reality—cannot come from nothing.

The truth of premise two, scientifically speaking, is largely based on the reluctant but eventual wide acceptance of "Big Bang" cosmology. Some Christians think the idea of a Big Bang is incompatible with the biblical idea of divine creation. Certainly, if one takes a "young earth" view that the Bible *requires* the creation "days" in Genesis to be 24-hour solar days and the universe is no older than about 10,000 years, then a Big Bang over 13 billion years ago is a threat to be thwarted.[88] However, even if one holds to a young earth view, I submit that Big Bang cosmology can still appropriately be used to make a couple of crucial points on which all Christians should agree: (a) the universe is not eternal and (b) the universe cannot explain itself.

One irony is that while some Christians think the Big Bang is *incompatible with* biblical creation, some scientists resist the Big Bang because it sounds *too much like* creation! Fred Hoyle (1915–2001), an atheist British astronomer who disparagingly coined the term "Big Bang," strongly rejected a Big Bang, in part because "the big bang [*sic*] theory requires a recent origin of the universe that openly invites the concept of creation."[89] It seems that 13-plus billion years ago is "recent" when compared to an eternal universe. John Maddox, a former editor of the prestigious journal *Nature*, said the idea of a Big Bang is "thoroughly unacceptable" because it implies an "ultimate origin of our world" and gives creationists "ample justification" for their beliefs.[90]

The scientific notion of a Big Bang has a fascinating history. Coming into the twentieth century, the dominant view among scientists was that the universe was eternal. However, repeated observations increasingly supported the view that the universe actually *began.* Edwin Hubble's shocking telescope discoveries in the 1920s revealed the universe is rapidly expanding—ultimately from some "singularity."[91] In 1965, Arno Penzias and Robert Wilson gave a significant boost to the acceptance of a Big Bang. They unexpectedly detected background radiation throughout the universe—a kind of cosmic residue that would have been produced by a Big Bang. Subsequent and more precise satellite observations gave further confirmation of a Big Bang. All of this points to a *beginning* to the universe.

George Smoot, head of the Cosmic Background Explorer project, said they had "found evidence of the birth of the universe. . . . It's really like looking back at creation and seeing the creation of space and time and the universe and everything in it."[92] And Alexander Vilenkin, a notable cosmologist, summarizes it this way: "There are no models at this time that provide a satisfactory model for a universe without a beginning."[93]

The universe *began.* That is not only the affirmation of Genesis 1:1, but it is also the consensus of current cosmologists. I like to put it like this: the Big Bang is an attempt to describe *scientifically* what Genesis declares *theologically.* What could have caused the universe to begin to exist? Arguably, whatever it is—or whoever it is—would have to be outside of time (eternal), outside of space (immaterial), and unimaginably powerful. This, as Aquinas repeatedly asserted, is what everybody means by "God."[94]

So what are the alternatives to a divine creator? Surprisingly, a primary alternative is that the universe was *not caused by anything* and it came *from nothing*! Vilenkin claims that "there is nothing to prevent such a universe from being *spontaneously created out of nothing.*"[95] Stephen Hawking, the late famous Cambridge physicist, argues that because there is a law like gravity, "the universe can and will *create itself from nothing.*"[96] And Alex Rosenberg, an atheist philosopher, exclaims, "Why is there a universe at all? *No reason at all.* Why is there a multiverse in which universes *pop into existence for no reason at all? No reason at all!*"[97]

The irony is that atheists often condemn Christians for not being scientific and for not being rational. But here we find atheists who propose hypotheses that have little, if any, prospect of ever being scientifically confirmed.[98] When I consider what needs to be explained—the existence of the universe—and I compare a Christian view of creation with the alternatives, I come away with a justified conviction—*a certitude*—about knowing God exists.

2. *The Design of the Universe Points to God.* The cosmological argument points to God's existence based upon the fact *that* the universe exists. Another kind of argument, called the *teleological* argument, addresses *how* the universe is.[99] When I refer to "how" the universe is, I mean it more in the sense of asking a teenager, "How is your bedroom today?" I want to know: Is it a chaotic mess or is it orderly enough that, if you look at it, you would conclude someone had put it in order? As applied to the universe (and countless things within it), the teleological argument contends the universe

possesses the kind of order or design that is far better accounted for by some vast intelligence (arguably God) rather than by mere accident or natural process.

A teleological argument was famously presented by William Paley (1743–1805) called the "watchmaker argument."[100] He argued if we found a functioning watch, we would rightly infer some watchmaker was responsible for it. In a similar way, the functioning design of the universe is best explained by a designer: God. Since the 1980s, another form of the argument (referred to as the "anthropic principle") has had enormous impact both on God-believers and those who are not. The anthropic principle focuses on the necessary conditions of the universe that allowed life to start *in the first place* and on how the universe can allow advanced forms of life, like humans, to exist.[101]

The "Goldilocks Principle" would be a simple way to think of it. Goldilocks experienced porridge that was too hot and too cold; chairs that were too big and too small; and beds that were too hard and too soft. But she also experienced porridge, a chair, and a bed that were "just right." In the children's story, the worst problem Goldilocks had was some discomfort and the bears. But as applied to the universe, if *everything necessary* for life were not precisely just right, Goldilocks would never exist!

One way to express a version of the anthropic principle is as follows: *The universe had to possess in its initial conditions (and in conditions since) precisely the right phys-ical constants in order for life, and particularly for human life, to exist.* A quick illustration might help explain: If the universe began with a Big Bang, the expansion rate of the universe had to be "just right" for life to exist. If this rate were too much, the universe would just fly apart and never form galaxies, star and sun systems, etcetera. If it were too little, the universe would have collapsed in on itself because of gravity. In either case, Goldilocks is in deep trouble!

Just how precise would the expansion rate have to be to make it possible for Goldilocks (and us) to live in this universe? The answer is that the expansion rate would have to be "just right" to the level of 1 part in 10 to the 55th power.[102] That means that if it's off by just 1 in 10 followed by 54 zeros, the universe would not have allowed any of us to exist!

The amazing thing is there are several dozen such physical constants that have to be mind-blowingly pre-cise for advanced forms of life to exist. These include the strength of gravity, the electromagnetic force, the density of mass in the universe, and many more.[103] The physicist Stephen Hawking summarized the point: "The remark-able fact is that the values of these numbers seem to have been very finely adjusted to make possible the devel-opment of life."[104] Roger Penrose, a Nobel Laureate in physics, described it in phenomenal fashion. He said if we tried to represent the improbability of producing "a universe compatible . . . with what we now observe," it would involve writing the number 1 followed by 10 to the 123rd power. To illustrate, if we wrote a zero on every particle in the entire universe, we would run out of particles before we could write the number![105]

It's easy to get lost—and perhaps confused—with all the numbers. The big point is this: both theists and atheists are absolutely amazed at these stunning and amazingly precise characteristics of our universe that made the existence of life possible. The atheist Fred Hoyle said, "A common sense interpretation of the facts suggests that a superintellect has monkeyed with physics, as well as with chemistry and biology."[106] The atheist Francis Crick, a co-discoverer of the DNA structure, conceded, "An honest man, armed with all the knowledge available to us now, could only state that in some sense, the origin of life appears at the moment to be almost a miracle, so many are the conditions which would have had to have been satisfied to get it going."[107]

Speaking of DNA, it shouts of intelligent design! DNA uses a phenomenally complex language to provide the specific instructions for twenty different amino acids to form long chains that become three-dimensional functioning proteins. Francis Collins, former director of the Human Genome Project, calls DNA "the language of God."[108] Stephen Meyer describes DNA as a "signature in the cell" that can only be produced by intelligence.[109]

The complexity of DNA is mind-blowing. A typical human adult has about 30 trillion cells with a DNA molecule. If one DNA molecule were uncoiled and stretched out, it would be about six feet long. That means that if the DNA molecules in one adult were all placed end-to-end, they would stretch out over 34 billion miles—enough to make 183 round trips from the earth to the sun!

However, the most amazing point of DNA is its *information capacity*. According to a 2017 study, one gram of DNA can hold 215 petabytes of information. With that capacity, DNA could physically store *all* of the information ever recorded by humans in one room![110] How did DNA acquire this capacity, and even more importantly, how did it acquire the information it possesses in order for life to exist and replicate?

How do we account for this spectacular "fine-tuning" of the universe and the existence of life? We could claim our universe is just one among an infinite number of universes, and we just happen to be in the one that's just right for life. But there are major problems with this view.[111] Or we could be compelled to acknowledge that a marvelously intelligent God "fashioned and made the earth"; "he did not create it to be empty, but formed it to be inhabited" (Isaiah 45:18b).[112] We could recognize the wonder of the psalmist who says, "The heavens declare the glory of God" and "day after day they pour forth speech; night after night they reveal knowledge" (Psalm 19:1–2).

When I consider what needs to be explained—the nature of the universe and life—and I compare a Christian view of creation with the alternatives, I come away with a justified conviction—a certitude—about knowing God exists.[113]

THE CHARACTER OF GOD

WE CAN ALSO KNOW truth about the *character* of God. Much of this truth is revealed in Scripture, but the nature of the universe, including our own deep sense of morality, also reveals truth about God's character. God's characteristics are sometimes described in terms of "incommunicable" and "communicable" attributes.[114] *Incommunicable* attributes emphasize characteristics that only God possesses. *Communicable* attributes are those that are shared with humans. God (and humans to some extent) are (or can be) personal, loving, faithful, holy, and wise. In this section, we'll just consider some characteristics that are unique to God.

Romans 1–2 offers a valuable backdrop for our knowledge of the unique attributes of God. Paul claims everyone, even those who do not honor God, has some knowledge of God's attributes from nature. He says:

> What may be *known* about God is plain to them, because God has made it plain to them. For since the creation of the world *God's invisible qualities—his eternal power and divine nature*—have been clearly seen, being understood from what has been made, so that people are without excuse. (Romans 1:19–20)[115]

While many Christians have heard about these attributes of God, they sometimes have a simplistic understanding of them that can harm their witness to others. So it is important to look a little deeper at what some of these qualities mean (and don't mean). The qualities discussed below are among the most prominent qualities of God that also tend to be misunderstood and theologically challenging.

1. *God Is Eternal, Immortal, and Self-Existent.* Scripture describes God as eternal. He is "from everlasting to everlasting" (Psalm 90:2c). He is "the King eternal, immortal, invisible, the only God" (1 Timothy 1:17a).[116] In other words, God is infinite with respect to time. He, unlike humans, is immortal.[117] He has no beginning and no end. He is *self-existent*, which means

that God's existence does not, and cannot, depend on anything else or anyone else.[118]

Properly understanding this helps us see why it is a mistake to ask, "If God made the universe, then who made God?" Initially, the question might make sense. We expect everything that exists in this universe must have a cause. But once we start the chain—"a" is caused by "b"; "b" is caused by "c"; "c" is caused by "d," and so on—we inevitably see the process cannot literally go back forever. There has to be something that was just there, or else the process never would have gotten started. Aristotle rightly acknowledged this by concluding there has to be some "unmoved mover" (God).[119] For Christian believers, the ultimate stopping point is the self-existent God, who is the only reality that requires no further cause or explanation.

Some critics might object and say to the Christian, "Well, isn't that convenient. You require an explanation for the universe and everything in it, but now you're just saying God doesn't need any explanation." The basic response is this: "You're correct. God needs no explanation. He alone is self-existent." However, the response should also include the following point: "There has to be some ultimate stopping point. One might claim that it's the universe itself. But that merely asserts the universe is self-sufficient instead of God." In other words, neither the Christian nor the critic avoids having an ultimate explanation. So when I compare a self-sufficient *God* to the prospects of a self-sufficient *universe* (which we know had a beginning), I have a justified conviction—a certitude—about which of the two makes more sense.[120]

2. *God Is Omnibenevolent (All-Good).* Scripture is filled with references to God's holiness, righteousness, and goodness: "There is no one holy like the LORD" (1 Samuel 2:2a); and this becomes the basis for God directing us to "be holy" because he is holy (e.g., Leviticus 11:44–45; 20:7; 1 Peter 1:15–16). The psalmist says that God's "right hand is filled with righteousness" (Psalm 48:10b) and that even "the heavens proclaim his righteousness, for he is a God of justice" (Psalm 50:6). Indeed, it is the *all-goodness* of God that makes the *grace* of God necessary for us.[121]

In addition, it is the all-goodness of God that makes the universal standards of morality and justice possible. In our world, we are overwhelmed by the cries for justice, human rights, and human equality—and rightly so. And these demands are seemingly made just as strongly by those who profess no belief in God as by those who believe in God. Why is that? I contend it's because there is a deep moral sense that some things are *objectively right or wrong.* That is, some things are right or wrong, independently of how we individually or culturally *feel* about them. The big question is: What is the *foundation* for our demands for justice, human rights, and human equality?

What are the alternatives? What entitles us to bring moral condemnation on acts of racism or any kind of injustice? Personal preference is inadequate; social custom is not sufficient; legislative dictates are inevitably deficient. What we need in order to justify our moral demands and criticisms is a moral foundation that is *universal*; one that *transcends* any human individual and any social or national group; one that is *unchanging*— even *eternal*; and one that is *all-good*. But those characteristics uniquely describe the God of Scripture!

When it comes to morality, it is the all-goodness of God that provides an argument for the necessity of God.[122] All other options to ground our universal sense of morality are destined to fail. But there is one superior option: "He is the Rock" (Deuteronomy 32:4a). *This* truth about God is proclaimed in Scripture, and it is also attested to in the deepest moral intuitions of humanity.

3. *God Is Omnipotent (All-Powerful)*. We can know from Scripture and from nature that God is *all-powerful*. Paul mentions that God's "eternal power and divine nature . . . have been clearly seen, being understood from what has been made" (Romans 1:20b).[123] Being "all-powerful" is often taken to mean that God can literally do *anything* and *everything*. And various passages seem to support this. Job claimed that God "can do all

things" (Job 42:2). When Mary heard she would bear a son, she affirmed that "nothing will be impossible with God" (Luke 1:37, NASB, ESV). Even Jesus said that "with God all things are possible" (Matthew 19:26b).

Such passages sometimes prompt critics to pose questions like this: "If God can do *anything*, can he create a rock so big that he can't move it? Can God create a square circle?" If Christians are not careful (or not prepared), they can be taken aback by such questions. I recommend the following response, though it may take some Christians by surprise: *God's omnipotence does not mean that God can do absolutely anything and everything.* He cannot make square circles, for example. As Christian philosopher Paul Copan explains, "No being, great or not, can do something *self-contradictory* or *nonsensical*."[124] C. S. Lewis put it this way: "His [God's] Omnipotence means power to do all that is intrinsically possible, not to do the intrinsically impossible. . . . It remains true that all *things* are possible with God: the intrinsic impossibilities are not things but nonentities."[125]

If this bothers you—that God cannot make square circles—it might help to think of other biblical passages that indicate that God cannot do some actions. Paul asserts God "cannot disown himself" (2 Timothy 2:13). The Hebrew writer says, "It is impossible for God to lie" (Hebrews 6:18). And James says, "God cannot be tempted by evil" (James 1:13).

The primary point about omnipotence is that *God can do anything he desires that is consistent with his nature.* He can do anything he wills to do, but God will never will to do anything contrary to his nature. This should be of great encouragement! God is good; God is faithful; and he will deliver what he has promised—because God has the omnipotence to make it happen. As expressed through Isaiah, God says, "My purpose will stand, and I will do all that I please" (Isaiah 46:10b).

4. *God Is Omniscient (All-Knowing).* Scripture proclaims that God is *all-knowing.* The apostle John succinctly says it: "He [God] knows everything" (1 John 3:20b). Throughout Psalm 139, David emphasizes God's intimate knowledge of who we are: "Before a word is on my tongue you, LORD, know it completely" (Psalm 139:4). God knows the count of the number of hairs on one's head and when a sparrow is sold or falls to the ground (Matthew 10:29–30). He not only knows what *does* happen, God knows what *will* happen. Through Isaiah, God says, "I make known the end from the beginning, from ancient times, what is still to come" (Isaiah 46:10a). God knows everything in advance.[126]

> GOD CAN DO ANYTHING HE DESIRES THAT IS CONSISTENT WITH HIS NATURE.

One way to construe God's omniscience is simply to say: "God knows everything—period." However, while the sentiment may be a commendable expression of faith, Christians should avoid being simplistic about what omniscience means. For example, if God knows everything—period, then does he know what it's like to *experience* sin—to *be* a sinner?[127] Does God know what it's like to be a woman or to be Richard Knopp with a headache? I suggest that God does *not* "know" such things in the same experiential sense as individual humans do.[128] However, this does not deny God's genuine omniscience. He knows all truths, and he intimately knows us as persons; but this does not require that God has *experiential* knowledge of sin or of one's individual identity.

God's omniscience generates significant questions regarding the problem of evil, human freedom, and individual salvation. If God knew that humans would sin and would initiate rampant suffering and pain, why did he create us in the first place? If God knows what I am going to do, am I really free in what I do? If God knows *now* whether I will experience heaven or hell, what choice do I really have in the matter?

These are challenging questions that elicit varied answers by devoted Christians. Let's focus just on the matter of salvation. Many Calvinists contend that God's sovereignty and human sinful depravity require that God alone determines who is saved and who is lost. He "predestines" them. If someone comes to saving faith, it is only because God has "elected" them to salvation and given that faith.[129] According to this view, a primary claim is that God's election is *unconditional*; one's salvation does not depend on anything other than God's own eternal decree.[130]

Non-Calvinists, on the other hand, generally stress that God's election is *conditional*: "God predestines those who meet the gracious conditions which he has set forth";[131] and God's election of those who are saved (or lost) is based on his *foreknowledge*, not his eternal, unconditional decree. Romans 8:29 says, "For those God foreknew he also predestined." And 1 Peter 1 addresses "God's elect . . . who have been chosen according to the foreknowledge of God the Father" (1 Peter 1:1–2a).[132] One important point is that *foreknowledge* by itself does not have any *causal* effect. Merely knowing something in advance does not, by itself, cause anything to occur. Just because God knows something *in advance* does not mean God *causes* it.

In sum, we can know much about God's character from Scripture as well as from God's creation. These qualities not only describe an amazing God, but they also offer marvelous benefits to us. God's eternality and self-existence provide ultimate stability. God's complete goodness justifies and sustains our deepest moral intuitions. And God's omniscience in conjunction with

God's omnipotence provide enormous reassurance that God is providentially in control of our world.[133]

THE ACTIONS OF GOD

IT'S QUITE POSSIBLE THAT God can exist and have all of the unique divine attributes we've explored, yet choose *not to do anything within human history*. This is the view of *deism*, which says God exists as a powerful Creator but does not involve himself in this world. According to deism, God is only transcendent (above us) but not immanent (with us).[134] But the deistic god is not the biblical God. The God of Scripture has been patiently and persistently involved throughout human history. He has chosen to come to us. He is not merely *transcendent*; he is also *immanent*. He "became flesh and made his dwelling among us" (John 1:14). He appeared as "Immanuel," which means "God with us" (Matthew 1:23; cf. Isaiah 7:14).

This biblical view of God is also very different from *pantheism*, which says everything is God.[135] But if everything is God, then God does not exist as a transcendent being who is distinct from the physical universe. God *is* the universe; the universe *is* God.[136] In a sense, therefore, God is only immanent. For the Christian, however, God is both transcendent *and* immanent. Yet God's immanence does not mean, as in pantheism, that God just mystically permeates all space and time. It means God has acted in specific ways at particular times within human history. This is the uniqueness of the Christian message. It is a truth we can know with certitude because God has chosen to act *within* the universe he created.

Scripture uses various terms for God's acts—including "signs," "wonders," "works," and "miracles."[137] While the four terms carry different connotations, they generally designate what I will classify as *miracles*. Defining a "miracle" is not as simple as some may believe. Many may think a miracle is a "violation of the laws of nature."[138] But the Bible itself poses problems with this view. For example, the plague of locust (Exodus 10:12–15) and the big catches of fish (Luke 5:1–11; John 21:4–6) do not necessarily violate any law of nature; yet we properly think of them as miracles. Some may also think of miracles as supernatural events that are *exclusively caused by God*. But this is also problematic biblically because Scripture also attributes deceiving signs and wonders to Satan and to false prophets.[139]

To make some sense out of all this, it's helpful to (a) distinguish *different types* of miracles and (b) emphasize *various purposes* of miracles. Approaching it this way can enable us to understand why it is so difficult, if not impossible, to give a single definition of "miracle" that is adequate.[140] It can also help us be more effective in our presentation and defense of Christian truth when we talk to others about miracles.

1. *Different Types of Miracles.* Not all miracles are alike.[141] So what are the different types? I think it's useful to distinguish *five types of miracles*: (1) creational miracles; (2) sustaining miracles; (3) providential miracles; (4) predictive miracles; and (5) suspension miracles. The first type, *creational miracles*, are divine acts that bring things into existence—like God's creation of the physical universe.[142] God's creation of matter cannot be construed as suspending, much less violating, laws of nature because there were no laws of nature prior to the existence of the physical universe. Yet in a sense, the very existence of the universe and its natural laws is a miracle. As the psalmist says, "The heavens praise your wonders, Lord" (Psalm 89:5).

Second, *sustaining miracles* point to the ongoing operation of nature that especially allows humans to exist and flourish. God not only brings the universe into existence; he *sustains* it. Hebrews describes God's Son as "sustaining all things by his powerful word" (Hebrews 1:3b). And Paul refers to the Son as "the image of the invisible God" in whom "all things *hold together*" (Colossians 1:15, 17).[143] The Creator's sustaining miracles are ultimately responsible for the conditions and provisions that make ongoing life possible. In that sense, the birth of every baby is a "miracle," but I doubt any atheist would regard this as evidence of God. Even so, as a God-believer, I have a kind of certitude that God miraculously sustains the world around me and, more personally, sustains *me* (Psalms 3:5; 54:4).

Third, *providential miracles* do not appear to go against the normal operation of nature, but the *timing* of related events seems miraculous. Let's say I fervently pray for a new job, and three minutes after the "amen" I receive an email with an exciting job offer. Is it a "miracle"? It *could* be, but we should be cautious against claiming too much about coincidences. Even so, consider an incident with Jesus. Accused of not paying the temple tax, Jesus told Peter to go fishing: "Take the first fish you catch; open its mouth and you will find a four-drachma coin" (Matthew 17:27b). This was certainly a miracle *because of the timing* between what Jesus said and what then occurred. In a sense, it was a coincidence, but it was not just a coincidence. God acted.[144]

Fourth, *predictive miracles* arise from making accurate predictions that are not adequately explainable by mere luck. Catching the fish with the coin (Matthew 17) was both a providential miracle and a predictive miracle. Jesus foretold what Peter would find in the fish's mouth. Predictive miracles were critically important in biblical history. A predictive miracle was a fundamental Old Testament criterion to distinguish between true and false prophets.[145] And the New

Testament highlights the fulfillment of predictive miracles.[146] Indeed, the NIV New Testament uses the word "fulfill" fifty-four times, at least thirty-four of which are presented as expressing a fulfillment of an Old Testament prophecy.[147]

Predictive miracles notably contribute to our knowing truth about God. God's power, his omniscience, and his faithfulness are manifested in the entire narrative of Scripture. Miracles are not merely extraordinary, isolated events; many are fulfillments of predictive prophecy. This fabric, which is woven throughout biblical history, helps us have certitude about God's actions.

Fifth, *suspension miracles* may appear to be "violations" of some natural law, but it's better to think of such miracles as "suspending" a natural principle.[148] Biblical examples include Jesus' healings and his nature miracles.[149] One important point about suspension miracles is that they were astonishing, *observable* events that offered truth about God and often authenticated a messenger of God. For instance, when Jesus healed the paralyzed man, he performed an *observable* physical healing to authenticate his authority to forgive sin—which otherwise would have been an unobservable act. It's also significant that Jesus wanted the miracle to grant *knowledge* of his authority. He said, "'*I want you to know* that the Son of Man has authority on earth to forgive sins.' So he said to the man, 'I tell you, get up, take your mat and go home'" (Mark 2:10–11; emphasis added).[150]

The most significant suspension miracle is *the bodily resurrection of Jesus*. In fact, the truth of Christianity depends on this historical event. Paul says, "If Christ has not been raised, our preaching is useless and so is your faith" (1 Corinthians 15:14). Without the resurrection of Jesus, Paul indicates that "only for this life we have hope," and in this case, "we are of all people most to be pitied" (1 Corinthians 15:19). It is therefore imperative that we examine the resurrection of Jesus. Was it really true? How can we have justified confidence in knowing this truth about God?

A comprehensive case for the resurrection of Jesus would require a sizable book, and many excellent works are available that provide impressive historical evidences and respond to various objections and alternative explanations.[151] For our purposes, I want to focus on a couple of considerations that especially help us have a justified conviction about the truth of Jesus' resurrection and the Christian faith as a whole.

First, the resurrection of Jesus was an *observable* event. At least ten different post-mortem appearances of Jesus are presented in the New Testament.[152] In addition, the resurrection of Jesus was publicly proclaimed, in Jerusalem where the event occurred, within fifty days of the event (Acts 2). And the disciples continued preaching the resurrection in spite of severe persecution and even death for doing so. (For instance, see Acts 4:1–22; 5:17–41; 7:1–59; 8:1–3).

Second, the resurrection of Jesus was an *unanticipated* event. The Greco-Roman and Jewish worlds offered no clearly understood theological, philosophical, or psychological basis for it. Pagan philosophies had dismissed the notion of an actual physical resurrection from the dead.[153] The Jewish doctrine about the resurrection only projected (a) a resurrection *at the end of the world* and (b) a resurrection that involved *everyone* rather than a single individual.[154] The Jewish view is illustrated by the conversation between Jesus and Martha at the death of her brother, Lazarus. Jesus told her that Lazarus "will rise again" to which Martha replied, "I know he will rise again in the resurrection *at the last day*" (John 11:23b–24). But Jesus transformed her thinking of resurrection only at the end of the world to a resurrection *in the middle of* human history: "I am the resurrection and the life" (John 11:25).

The Gospels offer no indication that the disciples of Jesus expected Jesus' bodily resurrection. Even though Old Testament prophecies foretold the resurrection, and Jesus taught his disciples about his impending death and resurrection (Matthew 16:21; 17:23; 20:19), John later wrote that at the time of the resurrection, "They still did not understand the Scripture that Jesus had to rise from the dead" (John 20:9). After the crucifixion, the disciples cowered in fear.[155] And it was only *after* Jesus' resurrection and their eyewitness experiences that they "recalled what he had said. Then they believed the scripture and the words that Jesus had spoken" (John 2:22).

All of this addresses a popular objection to the resurrection of Jesus—that it was fabricated by his followers. To put it bluntly: they made it up. But the basic point here is that the disciples did not have an adequate theological, philosophical, or psychological context to concoct the bodily resurrection of Jesus from the dead. They did not possess a sufficient framework to create what would amount to a "conspiracy" theory about Jesus' resurrection, and there was little basis to prompt a wished-for set of psychological hallucinations. Even so, hallucinations cannot account for the widely acknowledged fact that many disciples truly believed they saw a resurrected body on multiple occasions in different settings.[156]

2. *Different Purposes of Miracles.* In general, the Bible affirms that miracles are greatly intended to convey truth about God. And this can be more clearly recognized by understanding various purposes of miracles. How do miracles teach truth about God?

First, miracles *demonstrate* the lordship of the only true God. The Old Testament repeatedly reveals that a fundamental objective of God's miraculous acts was so we may *know* he alone is God.[157]

Second, many miracles *substantiate* the specific truth that Jesus is the Messiah (Christ), the Son of God. Jesus himself expressed that his "works" testify of him. He said, "Do not believe me unless I do the works of my Father. But if I do them, even though you do not believe me, believe the works, *that you may know and understand* that the Father is in me, and I in the Father" (John 10:37–38).[158] These substantiation miracles give us a strong case for knowing this truth about God and his incarnation in the flesh.[159]

Third, miracles *authenticate* Jesus' apostles and preachers in the early church, which gives us a foundation for having certitude about what they proclaimed. Miracles attended the preaching of Peter on Pentecost (Acts 2:43), of Peter and John (Acts 4:29–31), of the apostles (Acts 5:12), of Stephen (Acts 6:8), of Philip (Acts 8:6–7), and of Paul and Barnabas (Acts 14:3). Specifically, Acts 14 says the Lord "confirmed the message of his grace by enabling them [Paul and Barnabas] to perform signs and wonders" (14:3b).[160]

As we reflect on the actions of God, we see the various *types* of miracles were designed, in great part, for us to know truth about God. They exhibit truth about God's acts in the Old Testament, truth about Jesus, and truth about the message of Jesus as it was preached in the early church. We also see that God's *purposes* for miracles convey a confidence in their historicity. We can justifiably believe them to be true because they attest to God's appointed prophets and to the authority of the biblical narrative. As a result, knowing about God's actions should stimulate us to have greater courage in our witness.[161] In particular, the miracle of Jesus' resurrection is the primary incentive for boldly sharing the gospel with the entire world: "You are witnesses of these things" (Luke 24:48).

THE WORD OF GOD

IN ADDITION TO KNOWING truth about the existence of God, the character of God, and the acts of God, we can also know truth about the word of God. Biblically speaking, "word of God" refers to a message revealed by God, the Scriptures inspired by God, and the Son given by God.

1. *The Message Revealed by God.* While some truth can be known about God through God's *general* revelation in nature, much truth can be known about God through his *special* revelation: God has spoken in a variety of ways. The Hebrew writer says, "In the past God spoke to our ancestors through the prophets at many times and in various ways" (Hebrews 1:1). Sometimes God used *physical things* as a medium for his message. He spoke through a burning bush to Moses (Exodus 3),[162] through the Urim and Thummim to the

high priest (Exodus 28:29–30),[163] and even through a donkey (Numbers 22:21–38). Also, sometimes God used *visions or dreams* to convey his message. This included dreams or visions to those who were believers in God and even to those who were not.[164] At other times, God used *angels* to communicate his message.[165]

In most cases in Scripture, the phrase "word(s) of God" refers to the *content* of a message from God, not a set of existing writings.[166] Paul clearly distinguishes it from *human* words: "When you received the word of God, which you heard from us, you accepted it not as a human word, but as it actually is, the word of God, which is indeed at work in you who believe" (1 Thessalonians 2:13). This word is "alive and active" (Hebrews 4:12). It is the "sword of the Spirit" (Ephesians 6:17) that enables us to be born again (1 Peter 1:23). This word is the message that Paul charges Timothy (and us) to "preach" (2 Timothy 4:2).[167]

2. *The Scripture Inspired by God.* Although the "word of God" often refers to the *content* of God's message, it is also expressed in *written* form that possesses divine authority.[168] Jesus directly connected "the word of God" and "Scripture" when he cited what was written in Psalm 82:6. He said, "If he called them 'gods,' to whom the word of God came—and Scripture cannot be set aside" (John 10:35). Jesus notably acknowledged the authority of what was *written*.[169]

Various New Testament authors also stress the authority of what was *written*. According to Luke, Peter said "the Scripture had to be fulfilled in which the Holy Spirit spoke long ago through David concerning Judas" (Acts 1:16b). Paul says, "All Scripture is God-breathed" (2 Timothy 3:16).[170] And Peter contends, "No prophecy of Scripture came about by the prophet's own interpretation of things. For prophecy never had its origin in the human will, but prophets, though human, spoke from God as they were carried along by the Holy Spirit" (2 Peter 1:20–21).[171] These passages connect the word of God to Scripture, which derives its authority from God, whose Spirit animates and works in conjunction with human authors.[172]

Let's draw two important applications from this discussion on Scripture. First, we can know truth *about* the written word of God. We can study it, and it communicates truth about God. But second, we can know truth *from* the written word of God when we allow it to communicate truth *about us* and *for us*.[173] It describes our wretched human sinfulness and God's patient and persistent plan of salvation. And Scripture provides truth for how we *should* live, because it is "useful for teaching, rebuking, correcting and training in righteousness, so that the servant of God may be thoroughly equipped for every good work" (2 Timothy 3:16b–17).[174]

3. *The Son Given by God.* While it is important to see Scripture as the "word of God," it's also critical to understand that the ultimate word of God is a *person*, not a book.[175] John clearly makes this point when he speaks of the *logos*: "In the beginning was the Word [*logos*], and the Word [*logos*] was with God, and the Word [*logos*] was God. . . . The Word [*logos*] became flesh and made his dwelling among us. We have seen his glory, the glory of the one and only Son, who came from the Father, full of grace and truth" (John 1:1, 14).[176]

John emphasizes that the *logos* is not just *a* word; he is *the* word, who is eternal (1:2), who is God (1:1), who is Creator (1:3), and who becomes flesh (1:14). This *logos* is not an abstract mysterious force that pervades the universe; he is *personal*. This *logos* is not a distant, disinterested deity; he is "the one and only Son" of God (1:14b), who came to earth to make the Father "known" to us (1:18).[177] He is the one who came "to save the world" (John 3:17b).

> THE ULTIMATE WORD OF GOD IS A PERSON, NOT A BOOK.

Various New Testament passages provide truth about the Son who was given by God. Paul describes the Son as "the image of the invisible God" (Colossians 1:15; see also 2 Corinthians 4:4). The Greek word translated as "image" in these verses is *eikōn*. To illustrate the meaning of this word, every time you click on an icon on your mobile device or computer, you are clicking on an image that will open up some software application. I like to put it this way: "Click on the Jesus icon, and it will open up to God."[178] According to John, "The one and only Son, who is himself God and is in closest relationship with the Father, has *made him known*" (John 1:18b). Jesus is the "exegesis" or the explanation of God.[179]

The writer of Hebrews describes the Son as "the radiance of God's glory and the *exact representation* of his being" (Hebrews 1:3a). The Greek word translated as "exact representation" is *charaktēr*, which is an "exact reproduction of a particular form or structure."[180] One illustration of this is the typebars on old typewriters. Each typebar is a movable metal arm that has a small, molded character embedded in it. When a keyboard key is pushed, it causes the typebar to strike an inked ribbon and impress the character on the paper. Jesus is like that. If you push the "Jesus key," it will print "God."

No wonder Paul describes Christ Jesus as the Son whom God has exalted with a "name that is above every name, that at the name of Jesus every knee should bow, in heaven and on earth and under the earth, and every tongue acknowledge that Jesus Christ is Lord, to the glory of God the Father" (Philippians 2:9–11). *This* is the word of God who is the Son given by God!

THE POWER OF GOD

To REVIEW, WE CAN know truth about the existence of God, the character of God, the actions of God, and the word of God. But we can also know truth about God in an even more direct way: *we can personally know the power of God in our own life.* A prime biblical illustration is presented in John 9 with the man who was blind from birth. After Jesus healed him, a major theological debate ensued about sin, the Sabbath, and Jesus' identity.[181] Basically, the blind man said, "I don't know" about all that theological stuff, but "one thing I do know. I was blind but now I see!" (John 9:25).

This is direct knowledge, this is personal knowledge, and this is a kind of knowledge that cannot be effectively refuted nor easily dismissed. "I was blind but now I see!"—that should be the courageous confession of *every disciple* of Jesus. Even if we are not familiar with the theological, philosophical, historical, or scientific issues pertaining to knowing truth about God, we can know what God has done *for us.* Our "new life" is a life of immeasurable joy, knowing we have been completely forgiven of our sin by God's grace. It is a life of hope rather than despair. It is a life of ultimate purpose rather than pointless existence. It is a life made possible by the power of God through the indwelling presence of God.

Christians can know this "new life" by personal experience.[182] However, this is not merely some *subjective* sentiment like, "I feel refreshed today." It is not based on how we *feel* at any particular moment. It is a stable existence of newness based on knowing two *objective truths*: we are *in Christ* and God's Spirit is *in us*.

1. *Knowing We Are "in Christ."* First, we can know we are in Christ. The phrase "in Christ" appears over eighty times in the NIV New Testament epistles. Many instances make the point that because we are "in Christ," we have this new life. For example, "If anyone is *in Christ*, the new creation has come: The old has gone, the new is here!" (2 Corinthians 5:17). God reconciled "the world to himself *in Christ*, not counting people's sins against them" (2 Corinthians 5:19). "There is now no condemnation for those who are *in Christ* Jesus" (Romans 8:1).[183] We have "new life" *in Christ*! This is knowing the power of God. And this is worth sharing. As the angel said—the one who miraculously opened the jail doors and let the imprisoned apostles out—"Go, stand in the temple courts . . . and tell the people all about this new life" (Acts 5:20).

2. *Knowing the Holy Spirit Is in Us.* Second, we can know God's Spirit is *in us*. Jesus promised this just before his death. He said that the "Spirit of truth . . . lives with you and will be in you" (John 14:17). He said his Father "will send" the Holy Spirit "in my name" (John 14:26a;

cf. John 15:26). And on Pentecost about fifty days later, the apostles were miraculously "filled with the Holy Spirit" (see Acts 2:1–4). They preached the first post-resurrection sermon, which concluded with the command to "repent and be baptized . . . in the name of Jesus Christ for the forgiveness of your sins. And you will receive the gift of the Holy Spirit" (Acts 2:38). This "gift of the Holy Spirit" should be seen as God's indwelling presence that seals us with a divine guarantee that we are God's possession and that we have assurance of our inheritance in Christ.[184]

Paul talks about how we are "marked in him [in Christ] with a *seal*, the promised Holy Spirit, who is a *deposit guaranteeing* our inheritance until the redemption of those who are God's possession" (Ephesians 1:13–14). The Holy Spirit is a "seal"[185] that "guarantees"[186] our inheritance. The picture is that the gift of the Holy Spirit is God's *guaranteeing deposit* that everything promised is coming!

The gift of the Holy Spirit provides an *internal witness* for us (2 Timothy 1:14; Romans 8:11a). This indwelling Spirit produces a variety of marvelous benefits for the Christian believer.

1. He offers God's guarantee of our inheritance (Ephesians 1:13–14; 2 Corinthians 1:22; 5:5).

2. He provides God's promise of our own bodily resurrection (Romans 8:11).

3. He confirms our identity as God's children (Romans 8:16).

4. He creates a special intimacy with God that allows us to call him "Abba, Father" and makes us "sons," not "slaves" (Galatians 4:6; Romans 8:15).[187]

5. He empowers us to live a new life with hope and conviction (Romans 15:13; 1 Thessalonians 1:5).

6. He "does not make us timid, but gives us power, love and self-discipline" (2 Timothy 1:7).

7. He enables us to "walk by the Spirit" and to bear "the fruit of the Spirit" (Galatians 5:16, 22–25).

From these points, we can see how the indwelling Holy Spirit significantly contributes to our *knowledge*. Through him, we can know, in a more direct experiential way, our identity as God's children and our intimacy with God. We can have greater confidence in everything God's message of hope provides. And we can live a new life with the conviction that God's power is present.

How can we know all of this? The apostle John summarizes it this way: "This is how we know that he lives in us: We know it by the Spirit he gave us" (1 John 3:24b; cf. 4:13). By his Spirit, we can know truth about the power of God!

REFLECTION & DISCUSSION QUESTIONS

1. What is the difference between intellectual certainty and certitude? Why is this distinction important?

2. Can you restate the *Kalam* cosmological argument? How can this argument be helpful?

3. What considerations or illustrations in this chapter were most beneficial to you in pointing to the truth of God's existence? How so?

_____

_____

_____

_____

_____

4. Several aspects of God's character were discussed (e.g., eternal, all-good, all-powerful, and all-knowing). Try to explain some of these qualities in a way that a non-Christian could understand. What did you find especially helpful? Did anything challenge what you thought before reading this chapter?

_____

_____

_____

_____

_____

_____

5. In your own words, describe a notable idea about "miracles" that was presented in this chapter.

_____

_____

_____

_____

_____

6. This chapter discussed knowing truth about the existence of God, the character of God, the acts of God, the word of God, and the power of God. Explain one highlight that was especially insightful or impactful for you.

_____

_____

_____

_____

_____

_____

CONCLUSION

I n this book, I began by discussing the Bible's perspective on the nature of truth and the importance of defending it, especially in response to various philosophical and cultural challenges. Then I addressed two basic questions: "How can we know truth about God?" and "What truth can we know about God?" I ended by proposing we can know truth about the existence of God, the character of God, the actions of God, the word of God, and the power of God.

Atheists and agnostics reject the possibility of knowing any truth about God. Atheists simply deny God exists, and agnostics claim we cannot know enough to decide whether or not God exists. I emphasized that knowing truth about God does not require us to have absolute intellectual certainty. Instead, we can have *certitude* (or justified conviction) based on a wide variety of considerations that our core Christian beliefs about God are true. And I indicated that the God-less answers to the big questions of human existence are, by comparison, less adequate evidentially and less appealing existentially.

Even so, knowing truth *about* God is not nearly enough; we are called to *know God*. Jesus put it well in his prayer to the Father, "Now this is eternal life: that they know you, the only true God, and Jesus Christ, whom you have sent" (John 17:3). It's not a mere matter of knowing truths or facts about God; it's not a mere matter of mentally accepting truths about who Jesus was or is (Matthew 16:16) or about repentance or faith or the resurrection of the dead or eternal judgment (Hebrews 6:1–2). Knowing truth *about* God must drive us to *know God*.

J. I. Packer elucidates how we can do this in his classic work *Knowing God*. He writes, "How can we turn our knowledge *about God* into knowledge *of* God? The rule for doing this is demanding, but simple. It is that we turn each truth that we learn *about* God into matter for meditation *before* God, leading to prayer and praise *to* God."[188] Knowing God calls us to a personal relationship. It calls us to a life of loving God and loving others. It calls us to faithful obedience. It calls us to sacrificial service. It calls us to devoted discipleship.

> KNOWING TRUTH ABOUT GOD MUST DRIVE US TO KNOW GOD.

APPENDIX A

BOOK RECOMMENDATIONS FOR FURTHER STUDY

Paul Copan, *Loving Wisdom: A Guide to Philosophy and Christian Faith*, 2nd ed. (Grand Rapids: Eerdmans, 2020).

Timothy Keller, *Making Sense of God: An Invitation to the Skeptical* (New York: Viking, 2016). Book review by Richard Knopp at https://christianstandard.com/2017/02/helping-the-skeptical-see-god/.

Alister McGrath, *Mere Apologetics: How to Help Seekers and Skeptics Find Faith* (Grand Rapids: Baker, 2012).

J. P. Moreland, *Love Your God with All Your Mind: The Role of Reason in the Life of the Soul*, rev. ed. (Colorado Springs: NavPress, 2012).

Doug Powell, *Holman QuickSource Guide to Christian Apologetics* (Nashville: B&H Academic, 2006).

Room For Doubt, "Why Do You Still Believe?" Animated video at https://vimeo.com/327406232 and other resources at https://www.roomfordoubt.com/recommended-resources/.

APPENDIX B

RENEW.ORG NETWORK LEADERS' VALUES AND FAITH STATEMENTS

Mission: We Renew the Teachings of Jesus to Fuel Disciple Making

Vision: A collaborative network equipping millions of disciples, disciple makers, and church planters among all ethnicities.

SEVEN VALUES

RENEWAL IN THE BIBLE and in history follows a discernible outline that can be summarized by seven key elements. We champion these elements as our core values. They are listed in a sequential pattern that is typical of renewal, and it all starts with God.

1. *Renewing by God's Spirit.* We believe that God is the author of renewal and that he invites us to access and join him through prayer and fasting for the Holy Spirit's work of renewal.
2. *Following God's Word.* We learn the ways of God with lasting clarity and conviction by trusting God's Word and what it teaches as the objective foundation for renewal and life.
3. *Surrendering to Jesus' Lordship.* The gospel teaches us that Jesus is Messiah (King) and Lord. He calls everyone to salvation (in eternity) and discipleship (in this life) through a faith commitment that is expressed in repentance, confession, and baptism. Repentance and surrender to Jesus as Lord is the never-ending cycle for life in Jesus' kingdom, and it is empowered by the Spirit.
4. *Championing disciple making.* Jesus personally gave us his model of disciple making, which he demonstrated with his disciples. Those same principles from the life of Jesus should be utilized as we make disciples today and champion discipleship as the core mission of the local church.
5. *Loving like Jesus.* Jesus showed us the true meaning of love and taught us that sacrificial love is the

distinguishing character trait of true disciples (and true renewal). Sacrificial love is the foundation for our relationships both in the church and in the world.

6. *Living in holiness.* Just as Jesus lived differently from the world, the people in his church will learn to live differently than the world. Even when it is difficult, we show that God's kingdom is an alternative kingdom to the world.

7. *Leading courageously.* God always uses leaders in renewal who live by a prayerful, risk-taking faith. Renewal will be led by bold and courageous leaders—who make disciples, plant churches, and create disciple making movements.

TEN FAITH STATEMENTS

WE BELIEVE THAT JESUS Christ is Lord. We are a group of church leaders inviting others to join the theological and disciple making journey described below. We want to trust and follow Jesus Christ to the glory of God the Father in the power of the Holy Spirit. We are committed to *restoring* the kingdom vision of Jesus and the apostles, especially the *message* of Jesus' gospel, the *method* of disciple making he showed us, and the *model* of what a community of his disciples, at their best, can become.

We live in a time when cultural pressures are forcing us to face numerous difficulties and complexities in following God. Many are losing their resolve. We trust that God is gracious and forgives the errors of those with genuine faith in his Son, but our desire is to be faithful in all things.

Our focus is disciple making, which is both reaching lost people (evangelism) and bringing people to maturity (sanctification). We seek to be a movement of disciple making leaders who make disciples and other disciple makers. We want to renew existing churches and help plant multiplying churches.

1. *God's Word.* We believe God gave us the sixty-six books of the Bible to be received as the inspired, authoritative, and infallible Word of God for salvation and life. The documents of Scripture come to us as diverse literary and historical writings. Despite their complexities, they can be understood, trusted, and followed. We want to do the hard work of wrestling to understand Scripture in order to obey God. We want to avoid the errors of interpreting Scripture through the sentimental lens of our feelings and opinions or through a complex re-interpretation of plain meanings so that the Bible says what our culture says. Ours is a time for both clear thinking and courage. Because the Holy Spirit inspired all sixty-six books, we honor Jesus' Lordship by submitting our lives to all that God has for us in them.

Psalm 1; 119; Deuteronomy 4:1–6; 6:1–9;
2 Chronicles 34; Nehemiah 8; Matthew 5:1–7:28;
15:6–9; John 12:44–50; Matthew 28:19; Acts 2:42;
17:10–11; 2 Timothy 3:16–4:4; 1 Peter 1:20–21.

2. *Christian convictions.* We believe the Scriptures reveal three distinct elements of the faith: *essential* elements which are necessary for salvation; *important* elements which are to be pursued so that we faithfully follow Christ; and *personal* elements or opinion. The gospel is *essential.* Every person who is indwelt and sealed by God's Holy Spirit because of their faith in the gospel is a brother or a sister in Christ. *Important* but secondary elements of the faith are vital. Our faithfulness to God requires us to seek and pursue them, even as we acknowledge that our salvation may not be dependent on getting them right. And thirdly, there are personal matters of opinion, disputable areas where God gives us personal freedom. But we are never at liberty to express our freedom in a way that causes others to stumble in sin. In all things, we want to show understanding, kindness, and love.

1 Corinthians 15:1–8; Romans 1:15–17;
Galatians 1:6–9; 2 Timothy 2:8; Ephesians 1:13–14;
4:4–6; Romans 8:9; 1 Corinthians 12:13;
1 Timothy 4:16; 2 Timothy 3:16–4:4;

> *Matthew 15:6–9; Acts 20:32; 1 Corinthians 11:1–2;*
> *1 John 2:3–4; 2 Peter 3:14–16; Romans 14:1–23.*

3. *The gospel.* We believe God created all things and made human beings in his image, so that we could enjoy a relationship with him and each other. But we lost our way, through Satan's influence. We are now spiritually dead, separated from God. Without his help, we gravitate toward sin and self-rule. The gospel is God's good news of reconciliation. It was promised to Abraham and David and revealed in Jesus' life, ministry, teaching, and sacrificial death on the cross. The gospel is the saving action of the triune God. The Father sent the Son into the world to take on human flesh and redeem us. Jesus came as the promised Messiah of the Old Testament. He ushered in the kingdom of God, died for our sins according to Scripture, was buried, and was raised on the third day. He defeated sin and death and ascended to heaven. He is seated at the right hand of God as Lord and he is coming back for his disciples. Through the Spirit, we are transformed and sanctified. God will raise everyone for the final judgment. Those who trusted and followed Jesus by faith will not experience punishment for their sins and separation from God in hell. Instead, we will join together with God in the renewal of all things in the consummated kingdom. We will live

together in the new heaven and new earth where we will glorify God and enjoy him forever.

> *Genesis 1–3; Romans 3:10–12; 7:8–25;*
> *Genesis 12:1–3; Galatians 3:6–9; Isaiah 11:1–4;*
> *2 Samuel 7:1–16; Micah 5:2–4; Daniel 2:44–45;*
> *Luke 1:33; John 1:1–3; Matthew 4:17;*
> *1 Corinthians 15:1–8; Acts 1:11; 2:36; 3:19–21;*
> *Colossians 3:1; Matthew 25:31–32; Revelation 21:1ff;*
> *Romans 3:21–26.*

4. *Faithful faith.* We believe that people are saved by grace through faith. The gospel of Jesus' kingdom calls people to both salvation and discipleship—no exceptions, no excuses. Faith is more than mere intellectual agreement or emotional warmth toward God. It is living and active; faith is surrendering our self-rule to the rule of God through Jesus in the power of the Spirit. We surrender by trusting and following Jesus as both Savior and Lord in all things. Faith includes allegiance, loyalty, and faithfulness to him.

> *Ephesians 2:8–9; Mark 8:34–38; Luke 14:25–35;*
> *Romans 1:3, 5; 16:25–26; Galatians 2:20;*
> *James 2:14–26; Matthew 7:21–23; Galatians 4:19;*
> *Matthew 28:19–20; 2 Corinthians 3:3, 17–18;*
> *Colossians 1:28.*

5. *New birth*. God so loved the world that he gave his one and only Son, that whoever believes in him shall not perish but have eternal life. To believe in Jesus means we trust and follow him as both Savior and Lord. When we commit to trust and follow Jesus, we express this faith by repenting from sin, confessing his name, and receiving baptism by immersion in water. Baptism, as an expression of faith, is for the remission of sins. We uphold baptism as the normative means of entry into the life of discipleship. It marks our commitment to regularly die to ourselves and rise to live for Christ in the power of the Holy Spirit. We believe God sovereignly saves as he sees fit, but we are bound by Scripture to uphold this teaching about surrendering to Jesus in faith through repentance, confession, and baptism.

> *1 Corinthians 8:6; John 3:1–9; 3:16–18; 3:19–21; Luke 13:3–5; 24:46–47; Acts 2:38; 3:19; 8:36–38; 16:31–33; 17:30; 20:21; 22:16; 26:20; Galatians 3:26–27; Romans 6:1–4; 10:9–10; 1 Peter 3:21; Romans 2:25–29; 2 Chronicles 30:17–19; Matthew 28:19–20; Galatians 2:20; Acts 18:24–26.*

6. *Holy Spirit*. We believe God's desire is for everyone to be saved and come to the knowledge of the truth. Many hear the gospel but do not believe it because they

are blinded by Satan and resist the pull of the Holy Spirit. We encourage everyone to listen to the Word and let the Holy Spirit convict them of their sin and draw them into a relationship with God through Jesus. We believe that when we are born again and indwelt by the Holy Spirit, we are to live as people who are filled, empowered, and led by the Holy Spirit. This is how we walk with God and discern his voice. A prayerful life, rich in the Holy Spirit, is fundamental to true discipleship and living in step with the kingdom reign of Jesus. We seek to be a prayerful, Spirit-led fellowship.

> *1 Timothy 2:4; John 16:7–11; Acts 7:51;*
> *1 John 2:20, 27; John 3:5; Ephesians 1:13–14;*
> *5:18; Galatians 5:16–25; Romans 8:5–11;*
> *Acts 1:14; 2:42; 6:6; 9:40; 12:5; 13:3; 14:23; 20:36;*
> *2 Corinthians 3:3.*

7. *Disciple making.* We believe the core mission of the local church is making disciples of Jesus Christ—it is God's plan "A" to redeem the world and manifest the reign of his kingdom. We want to be disciples who make disciples because of our love for God and others. We personally seek to become more and more like Jesus through his Spirit so that Jesus would live through us. To help us focus on Jesus, his sacrifice on the cross, our unity in him, and his coming return, we typically share

communion in our weekly gatherings. We desire the fruits of biblical disciple making which are disciples who live and love like Jesus and "go" into every corner of society and to the ends of the earth. Disciple making is the engine that drives our missional service to those outside the church. We seek to be known where we live for the good that we do in our communities. We love and serve all people, as Jesus did, no strings attached. At the same time, as we do good for others, we also seek to form relational bridges that we prayerfully hope will open doors for teaching people the gospel of the kingdom and the way of salvation.

> *Matthew 28:19–20; Galatians 4:19;*
> *Acts 2:41; Philippians 1:20–21; Colossians 1:27–29;*
> *2 Corinthians 3:3; 1 Thessalonians 2:19–20;*
> *John 13:34–35; 1 John 3:16; 1 Corinthians 13:1–13;*
> *Luke 22:14–23; 1 Corinthians 11:17–24; Acts 20:7.*

8. *Kingdom life.* We believe in the present kingdom reign of God, the power of the Holy Spirit to transform people, and the priority of the local church. God's holiness should lead our churches to reject lifestyles characterized by pride, sexual immorality, homosexuality, easy divorce, idolatry, greed, materialism, gossip, slander, racism, violence, and the like. God's love should lead our churches to emphasize love as the distinguishing sign of

a true disciple. Love for one another should make the church like an extended family—a fellowship of married people, singles, elderly, and children who are all brothers and sisters to one another. The love of the extended church family to one another is vitally important. Love should be expressed in both service to the church and to the surrounding community. It leads to the breaking down of walls (racial, social, political), evangelism, acts of mercy, compassion, forgiveness, and the like. By demonstrating the ways of Jesus, the church reveals God's kingdom reign to the watching world.

> *1 Corinthians 1:2; Galatians 5:19–21;*
> *Ephesians 5:3–7; Colossians 3:5–9;*
> *Matthew 19:3–12; Romans 1:26–32; 14:17–18;*
> *1 Peter 1:15–16; Matthew 25:31–46;*
> *John 13:34–35; Colossians 3:12–13; 1 John 3:16;*
> *1 Corinthians 13:1–13; 2 Corinthians 5:16–21.*

9. *Counter-cultural living.* We believe Jesus' Lordship through Scripture will lead us to be a distinct light in the world. We follow the first and second Great Commandments where love and loyalty to God come first and love for others comes second. So we prioritize the gospel and one's relationship with God, with a strong commitment to love people in their secondary points of need too. The gospel is God's light for us. It teaches us

grace, mercy, and love. It also teaches us God's holiness, justice, and the reality of hell which led to Jesus' sacrifice of atonement for us. God's light is grace and truth, mercy and righteousness, love and holiness. God's light among us should be reflected in distinctive ways like the following:

A. We believe that human life begins at conception and ends upon natural death, and that all human life is priceless in the eyes of God. All humans should be treated as image-bearers of God. For this reason, we stand for the sanctity of life both at its beginning and its end. We oppose elective abortions and euthanasia as immoral and sinful. We understand that there are very rare circumstances that may lead to difficult choices when a mother or child's life is at stake, and we prayerfully surrender and defer to God's wisdom, grace, and mercy in those circumstances.

B. We believe God created marriage as the context for the expression and enjoyment of sexual relations. Jesus defines marriage as a covenant between one man and one woman. We believe that all sexual activity outside the bounds of marriage, including same-sex unions and same-sex marriage, are immoral and must not be condoned by disciples of Jesus.

C. We believe that Jesus invites all races and ethnicities into the kingdom of God. Because humanity has exhibited grave racial injustices throughout history, we believe that everyone, especially disciples, must be proactive in securing justice for people of all races and that racial reconciliation must be a priority for the church.

D. We believe that both men and women were created by God to equally reflect, in gendered ways, the nature and character of God in the world. In marriage, husbands and wives are to submit to one another, yet there are gender specific expressions: husbands model themselves in relationship with their wives after Jesus' sacrificial love for the church, and wives model themselves in relationship with their husbands after the church's willingness to follow Jesus. In the church, men and women serve as partners in the use of their gifts in ministry, while seeking to uphold New Testament norms which teach that the lead teacher/preacher role in the gathered church and the elder/overseer role are for qualified men. The vision of the Bible is an equal partnership of men and women in creation, in marriage, in salvation, in the gifts of the Spirit, and in the ministries of the church but exercised in ways that honor gender as described in the Bible.

E. We believe that we must resist the forces of culture that focus on materialism and greed. The Bible teaches that the love of money is the root of all sorts of evil and that greed is idolatry. Disciples of Jesus should joyfully give liberally and work sacrificially for the poor, the marginalized, and the oppressed.

Romans 12:3–8; Matthew 22:36–40; 1 Corinthians 12:4–7; Ephesians 2:10; 4:11–13; 1 Peter 4:10–11; Matthew 20:24–27; Philippians 1:1; Acts 20:28; 1 Timothy 2:11–15; 3:1–7; Titus 1:5–9; 1 Corinthians 11:2–9; 14:33–36; Ephesians 5:21–33; Colossians 3:18–19; 1 Corinthians 7:32–35.

10. *The end.* We believe that Jesus is coming back to earth in order to bring this age to an end. Jesus will reward the saved and punish the wicked, and finally destroy God's last enemy, death. He will put all things under the Father, so that God may be all in all forever. That is why we have urgency for the Great Commission—to make disciples of all nations. We like to look at the Great Commission as an inherent part of God's original command to "be fruitful and multiply."

We want to be disciples of Jesus who love people and help them to be disciples of Jesus. We are a movement of disciples who make disciples who help renew existing churches and who start new churches that make more disciples. We want to reach as many as possible—until Jesus returns and God restores all creation to himself in the new heaven and new earth.

Matthew 25:31–32; Acts 17:31; Revelation 20:11–15; 2 Thessalonians 1:6–10; Mark 9:43–49; Luke 12:4–7; Acts 4:12; John 14:6; Luke 24:46–48; Matthew 28:19–20; Genesis 12:1–3; Galatians 2:20; 4:19; Luke 6:40; Luke 19:10; Revelation 21:1ff.

NOTES

1. Cultural Research Center, "American Worldview Inventory 2020–at a Glance," April 21, 2020, https://www.arizonachristian.edu/wp-content/uploads/2020/04/CRC-AWVI-2020-Release-03_Perceptions-of-God.pdf. Data from a 2018 Pew Research study indicated that while 89 percent of US adults believe in "some kind" of God, only 56 percent believe in God "as described in the Bible," which refers to "an all-powerful, all-knowing, loving deity who determines most or all of what happens in their lives." Pew Research Center, "When Americans Say They Believe in God, What Do They Mean?" April 25, 2018, https://www.pewforum.org/2018/04/25/when-americans-say-they-believe-in-god-what-do-they-mean/.

2. Barna Research Group, "Tracking the Growth and Decline of Religious Segments: The Rise of Atheism," January 14, 2020, https://www.barna.com/rise-of-atheism/.

3. Barna Research Group, "Atheism Doubles Among Generation Z," January 24, 2018, https://www.barna.com/research/atheism-doubles-among-generation-z/.

4. See Kara Powell and Steven Argue, "The Biggest Hindrance to Your Kids' Faith Isn't Doubt. It's Silence," February 21, 2019, https://www.christianitytoday.com/

ct/2019/february-web-only/doubt-parenting-biggest-hindrance-kids-faith-is-silence.html.

5. The Room For Doubt program attempts to address the growing presence of skepticism and doubt in our churches and in our culture, especially among churched youth. See roomfordoubt.com.

6. David F. Wells, *No Place for Truth: Whatever Happened to Evangelical Theology?* (Grand Rapids: Eerdmans, 1993). Wells says, "The disappearance of theology from the life of the Church, and the orchestration of that disappearance by some of its leaders, is hard to miss today but, oddly enough, not easy to prove. It is hard to miss in the evangelical world—in the vacuous worship that is so prevalent, for example, in the shift from God to the self as the central focus of faith, in the psychologized preaching that follows this shift, in the erosion of its conviction, and its strident pragmatism, in its inability to think incisively about the culture, in its reveling in the irrational" (95).

7. Douglas Groothuis, *Truth Decay: Defending Christianity Against the Challenges of Postmodernism* (Grand Rapids: InterVarsity, 2000).

8. See A. C. Thiselton, "Truth," in *Dictionary of New Testament Theology* (Grand Rapids: Zondervan, 1978), 3:877–882.

9. Moses offered these instructions to Israel: "You must inquire, probe and investigate it thoroughly. And if it is true [*emet*] and it has been proved that this detestable thing has been done among you, you must certainly put to the sword all who live in that town" (Deuteronomy 13:14–15a; see also 1 Kings 17:24).

10. Thiselton, "Truth," in *Dictionary of New Testament Theology,* 3:881–882.

11.   The Hebrew word *emet* is typically translated as *alētheia* in the Septuagint, the Greek translation of the Hebrew Scriptures. The notion of "faithfulness," which is embedded in the Hebrew word *emet*, is communicated in the New Testament more by the *pistos* family of terms that denote what is faithful, trustworthy, or genuine (e.g., Luke 16:10–11; 1 Corinthians 4:2; 2 Thessalonians 3:3; Acts 11:23). See Roger Nicole, "The Biblical Concept of Truth," in *Scripture and Truth*, ed. D. A. Carson and John D. Woodbridge (Grand Rapids: Zondervan, 1983), 292.

12.   Nicole, "The Biblical Concept of Truth," in *Scripture and Truth*, 293. Nicole also states in the same source, "The primary New Testament emphasis is clearly on truth as conformity to reality and opposition to lies and errors" (293).

13.   Other sample passages that emphasize truth include the following: Paul reflects on the people of Israel and states, "I speak the truth in Christ—I am not lying, my conscience confirms it through the Holy Spirit" (Romans 9:1); Paul says he and his fellow teachers "do not use deception," nor do they "distort the word of God." On the contrary, Paul says, "By setting forth the truth plainly we commend ourselves to everyone's conscience in the sight of God" (2 Corinthians 4:2). Paul challenges Timothy to be a worker who "correctly handles the word of truth" (2 Timothy 2:15b), and he charges the Ephesians to "stand firm . . . with the belt of truth buckled around your waist" (Ephesians 6:14a).

14.   More literally, the Greek text says, "We are lying and are not doing the truth" (1 John 1:6, AT).

15.   John the Baptist "testified to the truth" (John 5:33), even though it literally cost him his head (Matthew 14; Mark 6). Jesus "told . . . the truth" that he had heard from God, which is why others sought to kill him (John 8:40).

Peter and others preached the truth and were threatened and imprisoned for it (Acts 4:1–20; 5:17–33). Stephen, the first church deacon, craftily integrated the narrative of Hebrew history with the unjustified crucifixion of the promised Righteous One, even though it led to his immediate execution (Acts 7).

16. Some suggest that using reason to defend God's truth is a *modern* concept tied to the eighteenth-century Enlightenment. This claim is unjustified and ignores the clear biblical emphasis on giving a reasonable defense.

17. See Acts 22:1; 24:10; 25:8; 26:1–2; 1 Corinthians 9:3; and 2 Timothy 4:16.

18. The emphasis placed on Paul's persistent *reasoning* with Jews and Gentiles is remarkable. See Acts 17:2, 17; 18:4, 19; 19:8–9. In Acts 19:9, the NIV only says that Paul "had discussions daily in the lecture hall of Tyrannus," but this diminishes the point that the ESV properly conveys: Paul was "reasoning daily." (The Greek word, *dialegomai*, is used here.)

19. For example, modern *culture* is characterized by a Western-dominated industrial economy (England and America); the social value of conformity; and a word-based, linear system of communication (e.g., a typewriter). Postmodern *culture* is expressed more by a global economy that is service-oriented; the social value of diversity; and a digital system of communication with images, videos, and emojis. The shift to a postmodern *culture* underlies the church's "worship wars" in recent decades. A search for "worship wars" in *Christianity Today* generates sixty-six items from 1996 to late 2020. For instance, note Megan Fowler, "Turning Up the Volume: Joyful Noise or Noise Ordinance Violation?" *Christianity Today*, March 2, 2020, https://www.christianity-

today.com/news/2020/march/church-worship-too-loud-noise-ordinance-violation.html.

20. I discuss this further in Richard A. Knopp, "Understanding and Engaging the 'Nones,'" *Stone-Campbell Journal* 21 (Fall 2018): especially pages 234–236. I propose that we use the terms "modern" and "postmodern" to refer to the respective cultural characteristics, and the terms "modernism" and "postmodernism" to refer to the respective philosophical ideas. One reason this is important is because I too frequently read or hear a Christian leader who contends that the church should embrace "postmodernism." But they are often just referring to how the church should change its methods to be more appealing to a postmodern culture. However, their terminology unfortunately implies an endorsement of the philosophy of postmodernism. Some go further and advocate that the church should adopt postmodernism as a philosophy. Examples of this latter approach are Carl Raschke, *The Next Reformation: Why Evangelicals Must Embrace Postmodernity* (Grand Rapids: Baker, 2004); James K. A. Smith, *Who's Afraid of Postmodernism? Taking Derrida, Lyotard, and Foucault to Church* (Grand Rapids: Baker, 2006); and Myron Penner, *The End of Apologetics: Christian Witness in a Postmodern Context* (Grand Rapids: Baker, 2013). While I believe philosophical postmodernism offers beneficial insights and valuable criticisms of modernism, in its stronger forms it is problematic for the proclamation and defense of Christian truth. In Penner's case, for example, he calls for an end to "apologetics," which he construes as "roughly the Enlightenment project of attempting to establish rational foundations for Christian belief" (ibid., 7). He claims, "Not only can apologetics curse; it actually is a curse" (ibid., 9; emphasis in original). I think Penner is

mistaken to characterize apologetics as an "Enlightenment project." As Chapter 1 indicated, apologetics, properly understood, is a biblical practice and imperative, not a concoction of modern philosophy.

21. See Groothuis, *Truth Decay*, 35–38.

22. This famous phrase is presented in 1637 in Descartes's *Discourse on the Method of Rightly Conducting the Reason and Seeking for Truth in the Sciences*, part IV.

23. For Descartes, a good God would not allow us to be so deluded as to have a clear idea of a tree in front of us if that tree did not actually exist outside our mind. This is why Descartes's argument for God's existence was so important for his philosophy. However, many critics were not convinced by Descartes's argument for God's existence. And without an adequate argument for God's existence, our knowledge of external objects is therefore threatened. If all we know are our own ideas (which was Descartes's view), how can we know that our ideas correspond to anything outside our mind, including God? As Kelly and Dew express it, "It is far from clear how we can get from this starting point [our own thoughts] to beliefs about the external world." Stewart Kelly and James Dew, *Understanding Postmodernism: A Christian Perspective* (Grand Rapids: IVP Academic, 2017), 244. On Descartes's "idea theory of perception," see J. P. Moreland and William Lane Craig, *Philosophical Foundations for a Christian Worldview* (Grand Rapids: InterVarsity Press, 2003), 148.

24. In a well-known passage, Hume said, "If we take in our hand any volume—of divinity or school metaphysics, for instance—let us ask, *Does it contain any abstract reasoning concerning quantity or number?* No. *Does it contain any experimental reasoning concerning matter of fact and existence?* No.

Commit it then to the flames, for it can contain nothing but sophistry and illusion." See David Hume, *An Inquiry Concerning Human Understanding* (1748), ed. Charles W. Hendel (Indianapolis: Bobbs-Merrill, 1955), 173; emphasis in original. The passage is from section 12, part 3.

25. Immanuel Kant, *Critique of Pure Reason*, 2nd ed., trans. Norman Kemp Smith (New York: St. Martin's Press, 1965), 29; emphasis in original. The quotation is in the preface to the second edition (1787).

26. Kirk R. MacGregor, *Contemporary Theology: An Introduction: Classical, Evangelical, Philosophical, and Global Perspectives* (Grand Rapids: Zondervan, 2019), 21.

27. See J. P. Moreland, "Four Degrees of Postmodernism," in *Come Let Us Reason: New Essays in Christian Apologetics,* ed. Paul Copan and William Lane Craig, 17–34 (Nashville: B&H Academic, 2012).

28. For some helpful Christian orientations to postmodernism, see James Sire, *The Universe Next Door*, 5th ed. (Grand Rapids: IVP Academic, 2009), chap. 9; and Kelly and Dew, *Understanding Postmodernism: A Christian Perspective*, chap. 1.

29. Groothuis speaks of postmodernism as "modernism gone to seed" because it carries modernism to its logical conclusion and inevitable demise. See *Truth Decay*, 40–42.

30. Modernism correctly speaks of truth that can be true for everyone. Jesus and the Christian gospel make this claim. Postmodernism rightly reminds us of our finitude and the role of our cultural and personal perspectives in how we interpret the world—and even the Bible.

31. The Christian philosopher, J. P. Moreland, poignantly describes this: "The secularized perspective is constituted by two worldviews—naturalism (fueled by scientism)

and postmodernism—that agree with each other . . . about one important point: *there is no non-empirical knowledge, especially no theological or ethical knowledge.*" J. P. Moreland, "How Christian Philosophers Can Serve Systematic Theologians and Biblical Scholars," *Journal of the Evangelical Theological Society* 63 (June 2020): 298–299; emphasis in original.

32. For examples, see Richard Dawkins, *The God Delusion* (Boston: Houghton-Mifflin, 2006); Sam Harris, *The End of Faith: Religion, Terror, and the Future of Reason* (New York: W.W. Norton, 2005); and Lawrence Krause, *A Universe from Nothing: Why There Is Something Rather Than Nothing* (New York: Atria, 2012).

33. Jean-Francois Lyotard, *The Postmodern Condition: A Report on Knowledge*, trans. Geoff Bennington and Brian Massumi (Minneapolis: University of Minnesota Press, 1984), 24.

34. Alasdair MacIntyre, *The Religious Significance of Atheism*, ed. A. MacIntyre and Paul Ricoeur, 14; cited in Alister McGrath, *Intellectuals Don't Need God: And Other Modern Myths* (Grand Rapids: Zondervan, 1993), 101.

35. Paine says, "The word of God is the creation we behold and it is in this *word* . . . that God speaketh universally to man. . . . The only idea man can affix to the name of God is that of a *first cause*, the cause of all things." Thomas Paine, *The Age of Reason: The Definitive Edition*, part 1 (Grand Rapids: Michigan Legal Publishing, 2014), 24, 26.

36. "Epistemology" is linked to the Greek word *epistamai*. A form of the word is used about thirty times in the Septuagint, the Greek translation of the Old Testament, and also in the Greek New Testament (e.g., Acts 15:7; 19:15; 1 Timothy 6:4).

37. The *correspondence theory* was classically expressed by Aristotle: "To say of what is that it is not, or of what is not that it is, is false, while to say of what is that it is, and of what is not that it is not, is true." Aristotle, *Metaphysics* 1011b25; cited in "The Correspondence Theory of Truth," in *Stanford Encyclopedia of Philosophy*, https://plato.stanford.edu/entries/truth-correspondence/.

38. The "pragmatic" theory derives its name from the Greek root *pragma*, which is used eleven times in the New Testament to signify the notion of "events" or "happenings." Luke uses the word to describe "the things [or the events] that have been fulfilled among us" (Luke 1:1). It is closely related to the word *praxis*, which pertains to action, practices, or deeds (e.g., Matthew 16:27; Acts 19:18; Colossians 3:9). See Christian Maurer, "Pragma," in *Theological Dictionary of the New Testament* (Grand Rapids: Eerdmans, 1964), 6:638–639.

39. Chapter 1 affirmed that truth in the Bible includes the idea of "conformity to reality in opposition to lies or errors." However, remember that truth is more than propositions. Truth is personal, and it even refers to a path or way of life. Jesus claims to be "the way and the truth and the life" (John 14:6).

40. Of course, we must clarify who "the Lord" is and what "risen" means, but it is clear from the biblical record that the reference is to Jesus who experienced an actual bodily resurrection after his crucifixion.

41. In 2016, the word of the year for the *Oxford Dictionary* was "post-truth." The adjective was defined as "relating to or denoting circumstances in which objective facts are less influential in shaping public opinion than appeals to

emotion and personal belief." See https://languages.oup.com/word-of-the-year/2016/.

42. For an informative and eye-opening discussion of how "post-truth" has affected our culture, see Abdu Murray, *Saving Truth: Finding Meaning and Clarity in a Post-Truth World* (Grand Rapids: Zondervan, 2018), 11–25.

43. Postmodernism raises a legitimate and perceptive point: truth is often little more than a power play. As James Sire says about postmodernism, "All narratives mask a play for power. Any one narrative used as a metanarrative is oppressive. . . . There is no purely objective knowledge, no truth of correspondence. Instead there are only stories, stories that, when they are believed, give the storyteller power over others." James Sire, *The Universe Next Door*, 225–226.

44. See James 2:26; Colossians 1:10; Matthew 7:16–20.

45. Plato presents his notion of knowledge as "justified true belief" (JTB) in his dialogues *Theaetetus* (202c) and *Meno* (98a). This conception of knowledge was nearly universally accepted by philosophers until 1963 when a philosopher named Edmund Gettier published a short article in which he described several somewhat odd but legitimate examples that showed it's possible for someone to have "justified true belief" without having genuine knowledge. Trying to resolve the "Gettier Problem" is still important to philosophers. Even so, Plato's notion of knowledge as "justified true belief" still rightly presents what is *necessary* for knowledge and, aside from some conjectured odd examples, it still poses a practical and acceptable understanding of what is *sufficient* for knowledge. For an excellent discussion of this by two Christian philosophers, see James K. Dew and Mark W. Foreman, "What Is Knowledge?" in *How Do We Know? An Introduction to Epistemology* (Grand Rapids: IVP Academic, 2014), 19–30.

46. This does not mean we only know things that are true. That would be ridiculous. Clearly, I *know* "2 plus 2 equals 5" is *false*.

47. In Plato's *Meno* (98a), Plato distinguishes genuine knowledge from true opinion. True opinions are certainly useful, but to have knowledge, one must "tether them *by working out the reason*" (emphasis added). In order words, one's opinion might accidentally be correct, but it's not real knowledge unless it has some justification or basis.

48. The scenario in *The Matrix* was raised over 350 years ago by René Descartes as he contemplated what an evil genius might do.

49. Those who disdain doubt typically point to various Bible passages. Jesus said to Peter when he slipped into the water: "You of little faith . . . why did you doubt?" (Matthew 14:31). He told his disciples, "If you have faith and do not doubt," you can command a mountain to fall into the sea (Matthew 21:21). And James says, "You must believe and not doubt" (James 1:6b).

50. This quoted phrase comes from Drew Dyck, who says of one study: "'The most frequently mentioned role of Christians in de-conversion was in amplifying existing doubt.' De-converts reported 'sharing their burgeoning doubts with a Christian friend or family member only to receive trite, unhelpful answers.'" Drew Dyck, "The Leavers: Young Doubters Exit the Church," *Christianity Today*, November 19, 2010, http://www.christianitytoday.com/ct/2010/november/27.40.html.

51. Two notable Christian philosophers say, "If someone knows something, it does not necessarily mean that the person has complete certainty about that thing." Moreland

and Craig, *Philosophical Foundations for a Christian Worldview*, 84.

52. As Christian philosopher J. P. Moreland explains: "When we seek knowledge of God, . . . we should not assume that our search requires reaching a state with no doubt, no plausible counterarguments, no possibility of being mistaken. When people believe that knowledge *requires* certainty, they will fail to take themselves to have knowledge if they lack certainty. In turn, this will lead to a lack of confidence and courage regarding one's ability to count on the things one knows. I am not suggesting that certainty is a bad thing— not for a second. I'm merely noting that it is not required." J. P. Moreland, *Kingdom Triangle: Recover the Christian Mind, Renovate the Soul, Restore the Spirit's Power* (Grand Rapids: Zondervan, 2007), 121.

53. Evans, *Why Christian Faith Still Makes Sense* (Grand Rapids: Baker Academic, 2015), 23–24.

54. Kinnaman points out that over 35 percent of young adults with a Christian background say, "Christians are too confident they know all the answers." David Kinnaman, *You Lost Me: Why Young Christians Are Leaving Church . . . and Rethinking Faith* (Grand Rapids: Baker Books, 2011), loc. 2120, Kindle.

55. Austin Fischer, *Faith in the Shadows: Finding Christ in the Midst of Doubt* (Grand Rapids: IVP Books, 2018), loc. 304–307, Kindle.

56. For example, when Jesus chided Thomas, the NIV translates Jesus as saying, "Stop doubting and believe" (John 20:27). But the context clearly suggests Thomas had *disbelief* in Christ's resurrection; he was not merely expressing some intellectual uncertainty. For this reason, the New American Standard better translates this verse, "Do not

continue in disbelief [*apistos*], but be a believer [*pistos*]"
(John 20:27, NASB). The Greek for "disbelief" in this verse is
present tense, and it simply adds a negation to the word *pistos*.

57. This distinction also helps make sense out of Jesus'
reaction to John the Baptist, who went from confident-
ly declaring, "Look, the Lamb of God, who takes away the
sin of the world!" (John 1:29) to the question, "Are you the
one who is to come, or should we expect someone else?"
(Matthew 11:3). John's circumstances had changed. He
was now in prison. He was no longer *absolutely certain* of
his claim; he had doubt. But he had not reached a point of
disbelief. As a result, Jesus did not condemn John's question
or doubt. After giving John further evidence to address his
doubt, Jesus went on to say that "among those born of wom-
en there has not risen anyone greater than John the Baptist"
(Matthew 11:11a).

58. Peter concluded his great Pentecost sermon by saying, "Therefore let all Israel be *assured* of this" (Acts 2:36).
The NASB says Israel can "know *for certain.*" The Message
translation even puts it this way: "All Israel, then, know this:
There's *no longer room for doubt*" (Acts 2:36). And Paul says
God has "given *proof* of this [coming judgment] to everyone
by raising him [Jesus] from the dead" (Acts 17:31).

59. Kinnaman insightfully suggests that the most dangerous doubt is "unexpressed doubt." Kinnaman, *You Lost Me*,
loc. 3088, Kindle. This is the motivational thrust behind the
name of the "Room For Doubt" apologetics program. Let's
provide room for doubt. See http://www.roomfordoubt.com.

60. Christians sometimes use the words "rationalist"
or "rationalism" in a negative way—as though these terms
necessarily mean that reason is used to attack religion or
Christianity. While this is appropriate in some contexts, as a

specific method of epistemology (knowledge), "rationalism" means reason can know some truth *without having to use sense experience.* If you believe that humans have a "built in" or "innate" knowledge of God, then you are a "rationalist" in this sense.

61. One of the major problems with a worldview without any God is how to explain the capacity of reason itself as a means to yield truth. If our minds are the evolutionary product of mere chance and purposeless order, why should we think that our minds give us *truth*? Darwin himself acknowledged this problem: "With me the horrid doubt always arises whether the convictions of man's mind, which has been developed from the mind of lower animals, are of any value or at all trustworthy. Would anyone trust in the convictions of a monkey's mind, if there are any convictions in such a mind?" See *The Life and Letters of Charles Darwin*, ed. Francis Darwin (1897; repr., Boston: Elibron, 2005), 1:285; cited in Groothuis, *Christian Apologetics* (Grand Rapids: IVP Academic, 2011), 414. For more cited references on this point, see Groothuis's discussion (ibid., 410–415) and C. S. Lewis, "The Self-Contradiction of the Naturalist," chap. 3 in *Miracles* (New York: Macmillan, 1948).

62. Using empirical experience to acquire knowledge should not be equated with the more specific philosophical view of "empiricism." Empiricism emphasizes that we have knowledge *only through sense experience.* The mind is like a "blank tablet" that has no innate knowledge; we have knowledge only when we receive sense experience. John Locke and David Hume are classic examples of this view. For Christians, it is important to understand that one can know many things from sense experience without going further to claim,

like the empiricists, that knowledge *only comes* from sense experience.

63.   The biblical references to God having hands, eyes, a face, and a mouth are "anthropomorphic" (e.g., Deuteronomy 11:12; 31:18; Job 33:26; 1 Kings 8:15; Job 15:30; Matthew 4:4). God is described as having a human form, even though Scripture is clear elsewhere that God does not have such physical characteristics (e.g., Exodus 33:20; Acts 17:29).

64.   I contend that biblical Christianity offers "empirical content" that vastly differs from other world religions and from some prominent theological perspectives within Christianity, such as existentialism and liberalism. See Richard A. Knopp, "On the Conceptual Relationship Between Religion and Science," in *Theology in the Present Age*, ed. Christopher Ben Simpson and Steven Cone (Eugene: Pickwick, 2013), especially pages 76–82.

65.   This kind of inference even occurs in science. Physicists infer the existence of things like black holes and subatomic particles like quarks and mesons—not because they can directly see them, but because of their measurable effects.

66.   Even though the apostle John acknowledges that "no one has ever seen God," two verses later he says that "we have seen and testify that the Father has sent his Son to be the Savior of the world" (1 John 4:12, 14). John uses the same Greek word for "seen" in both 1 John 4:12 and 14 (*theomai*).

67.   This is a primary consideration that prompted Alexander Campbell, an early leader in the Restoration Movement, to devalue religious emotionalism that was rampant in nineteenth-century America. He stressed "facts" and he pursued an "evidentialist" apologetic that begins with objective facts of history and the facts presented in Scripture. Campbell said, "All revealed religion is based upon facts. Testimony

has respect to facts only; and [in order] that testimony may be credible, it must be confirmed. . . . All true and useful knowledge is an acquaintance with facts. And all true science is acquired from the observation and comparison of facts." Alexander Campbell, "The Confirmation of the Testimony," *Millennial Harbinger*, 1st ser., 1, no. 1 (January 1830): 8–9. For more on Campbell's view, see Richard A. Knopp, "Lessons from the Philosophy of Science for the Restoration Movement Heritage (and Others)," in *Restoration and Philosophy: New Philosophical Engagements with the Stone-Campbell Tradition*, 121–151, ed. J. Caleb Clanton (Nashville: University of Tennessee Press, 2019).

68. What I discuss here about inner experience should not be identified as "subjective truth." Subjective truth, especially as it's popularly perceived, highlights the idea that a person *creates* truth or somehow determines what is true. I acknowledge that some truths may be thought of as "subjective." For instance, it may be true for me, but not for you, that chocolate ice cream is the best. However, my point is that some of our inner experiences (like our conscience and our deepest desires or needs) *can point to what is objectively true*. In this case, our inner experiences do not create these truths; they are used to *discover* these truths.

69. John Frame, *Nature's Case for God: A Brief Biblical Argument* (Bellingham, WA: Lexham Press, 2019), 48.

70. Jesus alludes to the conscience as a primary function of the "advocate" or "helper" (which is properly understood as the Holy Spirit): "And He, when he comes, will convict the world regarding sin, righteousness, and judgment" (John 16:8, NASB). The NIV translates the verse as follows: "When he comes, he will prove the world *to be in the wrong* about sin and righteousness and judgment" (John 16:8). But

this translation is problematic. It might imply, falsely, that the world is *incorrect* in its notions of sin, righteousness, and judgment. But the more proper emphasis is that the Spirit of truth will "expose" or "convict" the world (or the unbelieving person) of sin, righteousness, and judgment. In John, the Greek word, *elencho*, means "to reveal and convict of sin," which is also a key function of the conscience. See H.-G. Link, "Guilt, Cause, Convict, Blame," *The New International Dictionary of New Testament Theology* (Grand Rapids: Zondervan, 1976), 2:140–142.

71. The general point here is that there are *existential* reasons (as well as *intellectual* reasons) that point us to the truth of God. For a helpful analysis, see Clifford Williams, *Existential Reasons for Believing in God: A Defense of Desires and Emotions for Faith* (Grand Rapids: IVP Academic, 2011).

72. See the incisive assessment by Timothy Keller, *Making Sense of God: An Invitation to the Skeptical* (New York: Viking, 2016), especially pages 63–65.

73. C. S. Lewis uses the deep desire for an "unattainable ecstasy" in his case for the reality of heaven. See *The Problem of Pain* (New York: Macmillan, 1962), 144–154.

74. God spoke, for instance, to Abraham (Genesis 24:7; cf. Acts 7:2–6); to Moses (Exodus 19:19; cf. John 9:29); to David (2 Samuel 23:2–3); to Isaiah (Isaiah 21:16–17); to Jeremiah (Jeremiah 5:14); and to Ezekiel (Ezekiel 34:24). God spoke at the baptism of Jesus (Matthew 3; Mark 1; Luke 3) and at the Mount of Transfiguration (Matthew 17; Mark 9; Luke 9).

75. The New Testament uses the Greek word *mystērion* twenty-seven times. Paul especially emphasizes that "mystery" does not mean something that is *concealed*; instead, it is something that has been concealed but is *now revealed*.

Christ is "the mystery of God" (Colossians 2:2b) who "appeared in the flesh" (1 Timothy 3:16) and who is proclaimed (Colossians 4:3). Paul and others "declare God's wisdom, a mystery that has been hidden" (1 Corinthians 2:7; cf. Ephesians 3:9). The gospel is "the message I proclaim about Jesus Christ, in keeping with the revelation of the mystery hidden for long ages past" (Romans 16:25). This "mystery" has been "made known" (Ephesians 1:9; 3:3; 6:19; Colossians 1:26–27). Paul wants everyone to "understand" his insight "into the mystery of Christ" (Ephesians 3:4). See G. Finkenrath, "Secret, Mystery," in *Dictionary of New Testament Theology*, 3:504.

76. See Deuteronomy 13:1–5; Jeremiah 23:25–30; Matthew 7:15; 24:11; 1 Timothy 1:3–4; 2 Peter 2:1; 1 John 4:1; and Revelation 2:2.

77. As Campbell put it, such creeds are devastatingly divisive because they create "colored glasses" that prompt people to be "divided in their general views of Scripture." He continues, "One professor reads the Bible with John Calvin on his nose, another with John Wesley on his nose." Alexander Campbell, "The Bible," *Millennial Harbinger* 3, no. 4 (August 6, 1832; repr. Joplin, MO: College Press, n.d.), 343–344.

78. The theologian Alister McGrath explains a helpful distinction between "creeds" and "confessions." A "confession" (like the Lutheran *Augsburg Confession* or the Reformed *Westminster Confession of Faith*) pertains to a denomination and includes its specific beliefs and emphases; whereas a "creed" (like the Apostles' Creed or the Nicene Creed) pertains to the entire Christian church and offers "a statement of beliefs which every Christian ought to accept and be bound by." See McGrath, *Christian Theology*, 14. For an interesting

orientation from the perspective of the Churches of Christ, see Bobby Ross, "No Creed but Christ, No Book but the Bible," *The Christian Chronicle*, December 7, 2018, https://christian-chronicle.org/no-creed-but-christ-no-book-but-the-bible/.

79. Many in the Restoration Movement have little interest in church history. Somewhat ironically, many in Restoration Movement churches now exhibit a growing disinterest in the Restoration Movement itself. My plea is that we reconsider "why church history matters," as my teaching colleague puts it. See Robert F. Rea, *Why Church History Matters: An Invitation to Love and Learn from Our Past* (Grand Rapids: IVP Academic, 2014).

80. These four sources roughly correlate with a prominent emphasis in the Wesleyan heritage: the "Quadrilateral." According to McGrath, John Wesley (1703–1791) held that "the living core of the Christian faith was revealed in Scripture, illuminated by tradition, brought to life in personal experience, and confirmed by reason." McGrath, *Christian Theology*, 104.

81. In America, the percentage of atheists and agnostics grew from 11 percent in 2003 to 21 percent in 2018. Barna Research Group, "Tracking the Growth and Decline of Religious Segments: The Rise of Atheism," January 14, 2020, https://www.barna.com/rise-of-atheism/.

82. For a good discussion, see Paul Copan, *Loving Wisdom: A Guide to Philosophy and Christian Faith*, 2nd ed. (Grand Rapids: Eerdmans, 2020), 157–158, Kindle; and Alister McGrath, *Mere Apologetics: How to Help Seekers & Skeptics Find Faith* (Grand Rapids: Baker Books, 2012), 93–125. A valuable book by Stephen Meyer characterizes this as the God "hypothesis." Stephen C. Meyer, *Return of the God*

Hypothesis: Three Scientific Discoveries That Reveal the Mind Behind the Universe (New York: HarperCollins, 2021).

83. Copan suggests these pointers from nature produce, at best, a "thin theism" rather than "thick theism." Copan, *Loving Wisdom*, 158–160, Kindle. However, these pointers "at least present a reasonable basis for believing in the existence of a transcendent being" (ibid., 164).

84. The term "cosmos" is derived from the Greek word *kosmos*, which is used in 151 verses in the Greek New Testament. It is almost always translated as "world" (e.g., John 3:16, "For God so loved the world").

85. Aquinas personally believed the universe was not eternal, because God revealed in Scripture that the universe was created. But he did not think the *beginning* of the universe could be scientifically or philosophically demonstrated. So he constructed his cosmological argument on the assumption that the universe was eternal. See Aquinas's "five ways" to demonstrate God's existence in his *Summa Theologica*, 1, q. 2, a. 3 (available at https://www.newadvent.org/summa/1002.htm).

86. See William Lane Craig, *Reasonable Faith: Christian Truth and Apologetics*, 3rd ed. (Wheaton, IL: Crossway, 2008) and his website at https://www.reasonablefaith.org/.

87. Ibid., 96–97.

88. The issue about the age of the universe is contentious among Christians. One point to stress is that many devoted Christians who strongly advocate the truth and authority of Scripture see no problem with accepting the universe as being over 13 billion years old. Of course, this does not make this view true, but it does suggest we should be extremely careful about forcing others to think a "young earth" view is the only acceptable option for a Christian disciple. Personally, I

fear this is the dilemma some young Christians face: accept science and reject the Bible (which purportedly requires a young earth) or accept the Bible and reject science. See John Lennox, *Seven Days That Divide the World: The Beginning According to Genesis and Science* (Grand Rapids: Zondervan, 2011); and Hugh Ross, *The Creator and the Cosmos: How the Latest Scientific Discoveries Reveal God*, 4th ed. (Covina, CA: Reasons to Believe, 2018) along with his website at https://www.reasons.org.

89. Fred Hoyle, *The Intelligent Universe* (New York: Holt, Rinehart, and Winton, 1988), 237.

90. John Lennox, *God's Undertaker: Has Science Buried God?* Updated ed. (Oxford: Lion, 2009), 68; citing John Maddox in *Nature* 340 (1989): 425.

91. Most cosmologists believe they can use the laws of physics to calculate backward to this singularity to when the universe was just 10^{-43} seconds old. Beyond that, the laws of physics break down. Among many resources on this, one helpful description is Fred Heeren, *Show Me God: What the Message from Space Is Telling Us About God* (Wheeling, IL: Searchlight Publications, 1995), 114–126.

92. Cited in Heeren, *Show Me God*, 141–142.

93. Alexander Vilenkin, "Did the Universe Have a Beginning?" YouTube video, 39:32, http://www.youtube.com/watch?v=NXCQelhKJ7A. Cf. Alexander Vilenkin, "The Beginning of the Universe," *Inference* 1, 4 (October 2015), https://inference-review.com/article/the-beginning-of-the-universe.

94. See Craig, *Reasonable Faith*, 154. Cf. Aquinas, *Summa Theologica*, 1, q. 2, a. 3, https://www.newadvent.org/summa/1002.htm.

95. Vilenkin, "The Beginning of the Universe," https://inference-review.com/article/the-beginning-of-the-universe; emphasis added.

96. Stephen Hawking and Leonard Mlodinow, *The Grand Design* (New York: Random House, 2010), 180; emphasis added.

97. Alex Rosenberg, *The Atheist's Guide to Reality: Enjoying Life Without Illusions* (New York: W.W. Norton, 2011), 38–39; emphasis added. The "multiverse" idea is that there are many different universes, not just one.

98. For more on this, see Richard A. Knopp, "Where Will We Go Without God?" *Christian Standard* 149 (June 2014): 38–40; accessible at https://christianstandard.com/2014/06/where-will-we-go-without-god/.

99. The word "teleology" is derived from the Greek words *telos* ("goal") and *teleios* ("complete; perfect"). These words were widely used by the Greek philosophers. Plato and Aristotle used the terms to communicate the idea of a goal or completeness or perfection. For Aristotle, an acorn's goal (*telos*) is to become an oak tree (its *teleios*). See R. Shippers, "Goal," in *Dictionary of New Testament Theology* (Grand Rapids: Zondervan, 1978), 2:59–60. These words are also frequently used in the Old Testament Septuagint (246 times) and the New Testament (117 times). For example, we are to "become *mature*" (Ephesians 4:13); Paul wants to "present everyone *fully mature* in Christ" (Colossians 1:28); "solid food is for the *mature*" (Hebrews 5:14); and we should "let perseverance *finish* its work" so we "may be *mature* and complete, not lacking anything" (James 1:4). The NIV translates each emphasized word from a form of the word *telos*. The idea is that every Christian disciple has a *goal*—to become *mature*.

100. William Paley, *Natural Theology or Evidences of the Existence and Attributes of the Deity* (1802).

101. Many Christians rightly oppose Darwinism—evolution by *purely natural* processes. While responses to Darwinism are important, I believe Christians make a strategic error by not focusing more on an even stronger case: how life began *in the first place*. Darwinian natural selection cannot explain anything *unless life already exists*, so it's more important to press the point about the *origin* of the universe and the *origin* of life, especially to those who have no belief in any God.

102. Lennox, *God's Undertaker*, 71. On this point, Lennox, an Oxford mathematician, cites Alan Guth, a notable theoretical physicist at MIT.

103. For lists and a discussion, see Hugh Ross, "Astronomical Evidences for a Personal, Transcendent God," in *The Creation Hypothesis*, ed. J. P. Moreland (Downers Grove, IL: InterVarsity Press, 1994), 160–169.

104. Stephen Hawking, *A Brief History of Time* (New York: Bantam Books, 1998), 129–130.

105. See Roger Penrose, *The Emperor's New Mind* (Oxford: Oxford University Press, 1989), 445–446. The Christian astronomer Hugh Ross describes another astounding example: the *number of electrons* in relation to the *number of protons* must be accurate to 1 in 10 to the 37th power or better; otherwise, life would not exist. He graphically illustrates what this number means. He says to (1) cover North America with dimes stacked to the moon; (2) do the same with a million other similar-sized continents; (3) paint one dime red and hide it among all these dimes; (4) ask a blindfolded friend to select one dime. Now the question is: What is the mere chance that the friend would select the red dime?

The answer is 1 in 10 to the 37th power! Hugh Ross, *The Creator and the Cosmos*, 4th ed., 196.

106. Cited in Lennox, *God's Undertaker*, 70.

107. Francis Crick, *Life Itself: Its Origin and Nature* (New York: Touchstone, 1982), 88.

108. Francis Collins, *The Language of God* (New York: Free Press, 2006).

109. Stephen Meyer, *Signature in the Cell: DNA and the Evidence for Intelligent Design* (New York: HarperOne, 2009).

110. Robert F. Service, "DNA Could Store All of the World's Data in One Room," March 2, 2017, https://www.sciencemag.org/news/2017/03/dna-could-store-all-worlds-data-one-room.

111. One of the many problems with the idea that there are many different universes is that such a view is complete mathematical speculation that can never be confirmed by any scientific means. For a brief, relatively simple discussion, see Lee Strobel, *The Case for a Creator* (Grand Rapids: Zondervan, 2004), 138–140.

112. The physicist Freeman Dyson puts it this way, "As we look out into the Universe and identify the many accidents of physics and astronomy that have worked together to our benefit, it almost seems as if the Universe must in some sense have known that we were coming" (cited in Lennox, *God's Undertaker*, 59).

113. See the short video animation produced by Room For Doubt, "Why Do You Still Believe?" at https://vimeo.com/327406232.

114. See Michael F. Bird, *Evangelical Theology: A Biblical and Systematic Introduction* (Grand Rapids: Zondervan, 2013), 126–137.

115. Unfortunately, many people, while they possess this knowledge of God, "suppress the truth by their wickedness" (1:18), which includes "shameful lusts" (1:26) and "every kind of wickedness, evil, greed and depravity" (1:29). We might summarize Romans 1 as follows: (1) everyone has a *sense* of God, but (2) some *suppress* that knowledge and (3) *speculate* an alternative by exchanging "the truth about God for a lie" (1:25). In response, (4) God *severs* them by "[giving] them over" to their shameful lusts (1:24, 26), which results in (5) their *sinful* perversion.

116. Isaiah describes God as "he who lives forever" (Isaiah 57:15b). In John's revelation, God says, "I am the Alpha and the Omega" (Revelation 1:8; cf. 21:6; 22:13).

117. The issue of immortality as applied to *humans* is especially interesting. Plato thought the human soul is *inherently* immortal, and many Christians hold this belief as well. However, Scripture may not so clearly support this view. Paul refers to "God, the blessed and only Ruler, the King of kings and Lord of lords, who *alone is immortal*" (1 Timothy 6:15b–16a). For a discussion, see Tony Gray, "Destroyed For Ever: An Examination of the Debates Concerning Annihilation and Conditional Immortality," *Themelios* 21, 2 (January 1996), https://www.thegospelcoalition.org/themelios/article/destroyed-for-ever-an-examination-of-the-debates-concerning-annihilation-and-conditional-immortality/.

118. God's self-sufficiency is referred to as God's *aseity*, which means "God's all-sufficient greatness as himself without being tied to anything else." Bird, *Evangelical Theology*, 128–129. The very name of God delivered to Moses denotes this idea: "I AM WHO I AM" (Exodus 3:14a). As James Packer points out, "This 'name' is not a description of God, but simply a declaration of His self-existence, and His eternal

changelessness; a reminder that He has life in Himself, and that what He is now, He is eternally." J. I. Packer, *Knowing God* (Grand Rapids: InterVarsity Press, 1973), 69.

119. Aristotle discusses the "unmoved mover" in his *Metaphysics*, Book XII (especially 1072a–b and 1073a).

120. The section above on "The Existence of the Universe Points to God" explained that the *Kalam* cosmological argument only says that "whatever *begins to* exist must have a cause." It does not say that "whatever exists must have a cause." It properly excludes a self-sufficient and eternal God who can have no cause or explanation.

121. Paul says that "in the gospel the righteousness of God is revealed" (Romans 1:17). Indeed, this is the essence of Christian faith—that it is possible for us sinful humans to be declared righteous by a righteous God's grace on the basis of our faith in Christ and his death on our behalf (see Romans 3:20–25; 4:5, 24–25; 5:16–18; 2 Corinthians 5:21; Galatians 3:6; Philippians 3:9).

122. The "moral argument" for God's existence is powerful—for some, more potent than cosmological and teleological considerations. To illustrate, Francis Collins, who led the Human Genome Project, was once an atheist, but he claims that C. S. Lewis's use of the moral argument prompted his move from atheism to belief. See Collins, *The Language of God*, 21–22. Collins points to Book One in Lewis's *Mere Christianity*, "Right and Wrong as a Clue to the Meaning of the Universe." For more on the moral argument, see Room For Doubt's lesson on "Christianity: The Ultimate Basis for Justice and Equality," available at https://www. roomfordoubt.com/syf-curriculum/.

123. In 2 Corinthians, Paul uses the Greek word *pantokrator* to refer to "the Lord *Almighty*," which literally means

"all-powerful" (see 2 Corinthians 6:18). Paul is referring to 2 Samuel 7:8 where the Septuagint uses the same word—*pantokrator*. Accordingly, the NIV translates the verse with "Lord Almighty." (The NASB says "Lord of armies," and the ESV says "Lord of hosts"—which follow more closely the meaning of the Hebrew word *saba*.) "Almighty" [*pantokrator*] is also a core description of God in Revelation (e.g., "Holy, holy, holy is the Lord God Almighty, who was, and is, and is to come" (Revelation 4:8). For other uses of *pantokator* in Revelation, see 1:8; 11:17; 15:3; 16:7, 14; 19:6, 15; and 21:22.

124. Copan, *Loving Wisdom*, 117, Kindle.

125. C. S. Lewis, *The Problem of Pain* (New York: Macmillan, 1962), 28; emphasis in original.

126. God knew in advance the evil direction that the children of Israel would take (Deuteronomy 31:16–18). He knew in advance Jerusalem would be rebuilt and Cyrus would be used to accomplish it (Isaiah 44:24–28). He knew in advance Bethlehem would give rise to the "one who will be ruler over Israel, whose origins are from of old, from ancient times" (Micah 5:2b). It is clear that the first-century chief priests and teachers understood the Micah 5 prophecy to be about the birthplace of the Messiah (Matthew 2:3–7; cf. John 7:41–42). Micah 5:2 also implies the pre-existence of the Messiah, which John stressed (John 1:1, 14) and which Jesus affirmed (John 8:57–58).

127. 2 Corinthians 5:21 says God "made him [Christ] who had no sin to be sin for us." But God's imputing sin to Jesus does not mean that Jesus knew (*experienced*) sin in the same sense that humans do.

128. Paul Copan rightly says, "Insisting that 'God must know all things that humans know in the way that they

know' is nonsensical—metaphysically absurd." Copan, *Loving Wisdom*, 105, Kindle.

129.   There is no question that the concepts of election and predestination are biblical. The NIV uses "elect" or "election" fifteen times (e.g., Matthew 24:22; Romans 9:11; 11:7, 28; 2 Timothy 2:10; Titus 1:1; 1 Peter 1:1; 2 Peter 1:10). The NIV uses "predestine" four times (Romans 8:29, 30; Ephesians 1:5, 11), and the NASB adds Acts 4:28 and 1 Corinthians 2:7 to the list. The big issue is what these terms mean.

130.   Classical Calvinism uses the TULIP acrostic: total depravity; unconditional election; limited atonement; irresistible grace, and perseverance of the saints. See McGrath, *Systematic Theology*, 346–348.

131.   Jack Cottrell, *God the Ruler* (Joplin, MO: College Press, 1984), 338. Cottrell has several excellent sections that discuss sovereignty and free will (168–179); the views of "Christian Absolute Foreordination" held by Luther, Zwingli, Calvin, and Gordon Clark (71–83); and predestination (331–352).

132.   Cottrell claims, "The Bible explicitly relates predestination to God's foreknowledge, and a correct understanding of this relationship is the key to the whole question of election to salvation." Cottrell, *God the Ruler*, 341.

133.   God not only knows all truth about what *does* occur, he knows what *has* occurred, what *will* occur, what *could* occur, and what *would* occur (given the array of changing variables). As a result, he knows how and when to influence people and circumstances to achieve his historical and redemptive purposes. Cf. Acts 17:26–27; Romans 8:28–29.

134.   See the chapter on deism in Sire, *The Universe Next Door*, 47–65. Sire characterizes deism as a philosophy that

has a transcendent God who created the universe "but then left it to operate on its own." As a result, God is "not immanent." He is "only a transcendent force or energy" (51).

135. See the chapter on Eastern Pantheism Monism in Sire, *The Universe Next Door,* 144–165.

136. As Sire puts it, "God is the cosmos. God is all that exists; nothing exists that is not God" (ibid., 149).

137. Signs, wonders, and miracles appear together in three NIV New Testament verses: Acts 2:22; 2 Corinthians 12:12; and Hebrews 2:4. Signs and wonders appear together in thirty-two NIV Bible verses, with sixteen each in the Old and New Testaments. For Old Testament examples of the use of "signs" and "wonders" together, see Exodus 7:3; Deuteronomy 6:22; Nehemiah 9:10; Jeremiah 32:20–21; and Daniel 4:2–3.

138. This was the view of the skeptic David Hume. See David Hume, "Of Miracles," *An Inquiry Concerning Human Understanding* (Indianapolis: Bobbs-Merrill, 1955), 122. Philosophically, one of Hume's problems with defining a miracle as "a violation of the laws of nature" is that Hume's theory of knowledge cannot even justify the existence of necessary universal laws of nature in the first place. See Richard Purtill, "Defining Miracles," in *In Defense of Miracles*, ed. R. Douglass Geivett and Gary Habermas (Downers Grove, IL: InterVarsity, 1997), 67–68.

139. See Matthew 7:21–23; 24:24; 2 Thessalonians 2:8–9; and Revelation 16:13–14. The Egyptian magicians were able to replicate the first two of the ten plagues— turning water into blood and adding to the glut of frogs (Exodus 7:17–22; 8:5–6). However, Moses's staff becoming a snake suggests that miracles caused by forces other than God cannot ultimately compete with genuine God-miracles. The

Egyptian magicians were able to turn their staffs into snakes, but Moses's snake ate those of the Egyptians. See Exodus 7:8–12.

140. Win Corduan insightfully asserts that "any attempt to specify a convenient formula or absolute criterion for identifying a genuine miracle will only lead to disappointment." Winfried Corduan, "Recognizing a Miracle," in *In Defense of Miracles*, ed. R. Douglass Geivett and Gary Habermas (Downers Grove, IL: InterVarsity, 1997), 102.

141. Ibid., 103–106.

142. Creational miracles would also include God's creation of heavenly beings and realities, but here we will consider only creational miracles in the context of physical reality.

143. The Greek verb *synesteken* in Colossians 1:17 means "to bring together something in its proper or appropriate place or relationship." Johannes P. Louw and Eugene Albert Nida, *Greek-English Lexicon of the New Testament: Based on Semantic Domains* (New York: United Bible Societies, 1996), 613. This does not mean God holds things together in some physical sense, as though he were the strong nuclear force that binds protons and neutrons together. See "Strong Nuclear Force" at https://energyeducation.ca/encyclopedia/Strong_nuclear_force.

144. Ronald Nash refers to these as "coincidence-miracles." While he characterizes them as "apologetically inconclusive" (246), he says we can still cautiously construe them to support God's action in the world. See the excellent discussion in Ronald Nash, *Faith and Reason* (Grand Rapids: Academie Books, 1988), 244–247.

145. "'How can we know when a message has not been spoken by the LORD?' If what a prophet proclaims in the name of the LORD does not take place or come true, that is a

message the LORD has not spoken" (Deuteronomy 18:21–22a). However, making a true prediction is not sufficient by itself as evidence of a true prophet. God's law to Moses also says if a prophet accurately foretells some sign or wonder but also attempts to entice others to "follow other gods . . . [and] worship them," those prophets must be ignored (see Deuteronomy 13:1–3).

146. The birth of Jesus "took place to fulfill what the Lord has said through the prophet" (Matthew 1:22; cf. Isaiah 7:14). Jesus began his ministry by reading Isaiah 61:1–2 and saying, "Today this scripture is fulfilled in your hearing" (Luke 4:21). Jesus said to the two confused disciples who were disheartened by Jesus' crucifixion and who had not yet recognized his resurrected body, "Everything must be fulfilled that is written about me in the Law of Moses, the Prophets and the Psalms" (Luke 24:44b).

147. Peter interpreted what happened to Judas as a predictive miracle: "The Scripture had to be fulfilled in which the Holy Spirit spoke long ago through David" (Acts 1:16a; cf. Acts 1:18–20; Psalm 69:25; 109:8). The miraculous signs on the day of Pentecost fulfilled "what was spoken by the prophet Joel" (Acts 2:16). And the crucifixion and resurrection of Jesus were prominent predictive miracles preached on Pentecost (Acts 2:30–35). Peter later described what happened to Jesus as "how God fulfilled what he had foretold through all the prophets" (Acts 3:18; cf. 13:27, 33). Paul, in his defense of his conversion to Christ, explained to King Agrippa he was "saying nothing beyond what the prophets and Moses said would happen—that the Messiah would suffer and, as the first to rise from the dead, would bring the message of light to his own people and to the Gentiles" (Acts 26:22b–23).

148. For example, an airplane's flight does not violate the law of gravity; it uses principles of aerodynamics to suspend what gravity would otherwise do. Even the case of God raising Jesus from the dead can be construed as God suspending some natural processes through (a) other as yet unknown natural processes; (b) through God's more direct supernatural action in the physical world; (c) or both. One important point is that miracles, even if they are supernatural actions by God that intervene in natural processes, do not violate the principle of cause and effect. They merely acknowledge that God is a legitimate causal agent within time and space.

149. Jesus' healings include cleansing a leper (Matthew 8:2–3), healing a withered hand (Matthew 12:9–13), raising a widow's son (Luke 7:11–15), healing a blind man (Mark 8:22–25; John 9:1–7), restoring a cut-off ear (Luke 22:49–51), casting out demons (Matthew 8:28–32; 12:22), and many others. His miracles over nature turned water into wine (John 2:1–11), instantly stilled a storm (Matthew 8:23–27), and fed thousands (Matthew 14:15–21).

150. See Matthew 9:1–7; Mark 2:1–12; and Luke 5:17–26.

151. For an overview of sources on the resurrection, see Richard A. Knopp, "Resurrection Resources," *Christian Standard* (April 3, 2015), https://christianstandard.com/2015/04/resurrection-resources/. For a more current collection of relevant essays, see W. David Beck and Michael Licona, ed., *Raised on the Third Day: Defending the Historicity of the Resurrection of Jesus* (Bellingham, WA: Lexham Press, 2020).

152. These include post-mortem appearances to Mary Magdalene (John 20:11–18) and the women (Matthew 28:8–10); to Peter (Luke 24:34; 1 Corinthians 15:5); to the two on the way to Emmaus (Luke 24:13–32); to the Twelve, minus Thomas and Judas (Luke 24:36–48; John 20:19–22); to the

Twelve, with Thomas and minus Judas (John 20:24–29); to those at the Sea of Galilee (John 21); to more than five hundred at once (1 Corinthians 15:6); to James, the brother of Jesus who once did not believe in Jesus as Messiah (John 7:3–5; Acts 15:12–13; 1 Corinthians 15:7; Galatians 1:19; 2:9); to those at Jesus' ascension (Acts 1:9–11); and to Saul (Acts 9:1–9).

153. Various ancient religions characterized gods or goddesses as disappearing, as being assumed into some netherworld, or as symbolizing seasonal crops; but they did not present any precedent for an individual literally returning to *this* world of human experience after physical death. See Craig, *Reasonable Faith*, 390–391.

154. Ibid., 392–393.

155. For example, the disciples' fear is presented in Matthew 26:56, 69–75; Mark 14:50; and John 20:19.

156. See Zach Breitenbach, "A New Argument That Collective Hallucinations Do Not Adequately Account for the Group Appearances of Jesus in the Gospels," *Journal of the Evangelical Society* 62 (June 2019), 341–351.

157. The Egyptians "will know that I am the LORD" (Exodus 7:5a); Pharaoh "may know that there is no one like the LORD our God" (Exodus 8:10b; cf. 9:14, 29); and the children and grandchildren of the Israelites "may know that I am the LORD" (Exodus 10:2b). Later, Solomon said that God's mighty hand responding to prayers will even help the foreigners "know that this house [temple] I have built bears your Name" (1 Kings 8:43). And Elijah prayed for, and received, God's miracle at Mount Carmel "so these people will know that you, LORD, are God" (1 Kings 18:37b).

158. The healing of the paralytic emphasizes the same point. Jesus physically healed the man because, "I *want you*

to know that the Son of Man has authority on earth to forgive sins" (Mark 2:10a).

159. John informs us that Jesus performed "many other signs" that are "not recorded in this book" (John 20:30).

160. In addition, Paul uses his miracle-working to argue that he is "not in the least inferior to the 'super-apostles,'" because he "persevered in demonstrating . . . the marks of a true apostle, including signs, wonders and miracles" (2 Corinthians 12:11b–12). And the Hebrew writer argues that the salvation message, which was "first announced by the Lord, was confirmed to us by those who heard him. God also testified to it by signs, wonders and various miracles" (Hebrews 2:3b–4a).

161. That is what happened in the early church. See Acts 4:29–30; 9:26–28; and 14:3.

162. The instance of the burning bush is referred to by Jesus (Mark 12:26; Luke 20:37) and by Stephen (Acts 7:30).

163. While there are eight references to the Urim and Thummim in the Old Testament, we know little about them. They were apparently two or more small objects worn on the breastplate of the high priest that were used to signify God's response to specific yes-no questions. They may have been light and dark pebbles that were cast like lots. Though it appears to be a form of divination, which the law otherwise prohibited (Leviticus 19:26), it was sanctioned by God. See Allen C. Myers, "Urim and Thummim," in *The Eerdmans Bible Dictionary* (Grand Rapids: Eerdmans, 1987), 1032.

164. Notable examples include Abimelek (Genesis 20:3, 6), Jacob (Genesis 31:10–13), Joseph (Genesis 37:5–7), Pharaoh (Genesis 41:15–24), King Nebuchadnezzar of Babylon (Daniel 2:1–3), Daniel (Daniel 2:19), Joseph the husband of Mary (Matthew 1:20; 2:13, 19), and Peter (Acts 10:9–20).

165. The NIV uses the word "angel" 108 times in the Old Testament and 182 times in the New Testament. Both the Hebrew word *mal'āk* and the Greek word *angelos* mean "messenger." Those to whom God's message came by angels included Hagar (Genesis 16:7–12), Lot (Genesis 19:1, 15), Abraham (Genesis 22:11–12), Zechariah (Zechariah 1:9–21), the shepherds at Jesus' birth (Luke 2:8–15), Philip (Acts 8:26), Cornelius (Acts 10:3–6), Paul (Acts 27:22–24), and John (Revelation 1:1).

166. The phrase "word(s) of God" is used in the NIV five times in the Old Testament and forty times in the New Testament, including eleven times in the book of Acts where preaching is central. For example, the "word of God" was given to Saul through Samuel (1 Samuel 9:27), to Shemaiah the man of God (1 Kings 12:22), and to John the son of Zechariah (Luke 3:2). The people crowded Jesus, "listening to the word of God" (Luke 5:1b). The early Christian disciples "spoke the word of God boldly" (Acts 4:31) and it spread (Acts 6:7) and was accepted by the Samaritans (Acts 8:14) and the Gentiles (Acts 11:1).

167. The NIV properly translates 1 Corinthians 1:21 to say, "God was pleased through the foolishness *of what* was preached to save those who believe." The NASB is even clearer by referring to "the foolishness *of the message* preached" (emphases added). Somewhat misleadingly, the KJV talks about "the foolishness *of preaching*" as though the focus is on the style of speaking. Even so, Paul later emphasizes both his "message" and his "preaching" "were not with wise and persuasive words, but with a demonstration of the Spirit's power," so that their faith "might not rest on human wisdom, but on God's power" (1 Corinthians 2:4–5).

168. The word "written" appears 128 times in the Old Testament and 119 times in the New Testament (NIV). And the word "Scripture(s)" appears 53 times in the NIV New Testament. Almost all of these instances specifically undergird the *authority* and the *veracity* of the message. "It is written" (e.g., Matthew 4:4–10; 21:13; 26:24, 31; Mark 14:27; Luke 3:4; John 6:31, 45). The Scriptures "must be fulfilled" (e.g., Mark 14:49; cf. Matthew 26:54; John 17:12; 19:24, 28, 36; 20:9; Acts 1:20; 7:42; 13:29).

169. At least twenty-one times in the Gospels (NIV), "it is written" is specifically attributed to Jesus who uses it as an authority for his position. In Matthew, he used it in each reply to Satan's three temptations (Matthew 4:4, 6, 10). Interestingly in Luke, it is *Satan* who said, "It is written" in the third temptation, as though that would somehow prompt Jesus to yield (see Luke 4:10). Here, Jesus replied, "It is said" (Luke 4:12), which appeals to what is written in Deuteronomy 6:16. In another noteworthy verse, Jesus appealed to Scripture twice: "It is written: 'And he was numbered with the transgressors'; and I tell you that this must be fulfilled in me. Yes, what is written about me is reaching its fulfillment" (Luke 22:37).

170. The Greek word translated as "God-breathed" (NIV) or as "inspired by God" (NASB) is *theopneustos*. It is derived from the Greek words *theos* (God) and *pneuma* (breath or spirit).

171. Peter includes Paul's writings as authoritative "Scripture" when he says, "[Paul's] letters contain some things that are hard to understand, which ignorant and unstable people distort, *as they do the other Scriptures*, to their own destruction" (2 Peter 3:16b).

172.   Explaining the precise relationship between God's "inspiration" and what (and how) humans contribute to Scripture is challenging. Minimally, however, we should not think the exact vocabulary and grammar of Scripture are simply "recitations" from God (like Muslims believe that the Qur'an consists of direct "recitations" from Allah). Scripture is simultaneously both divine and human. Remember that Jesus was also simultaneously divine and human. For a brief discussion of various theories of inspiration and some helpful qualifications, see Bird, *Evangelical Theology*, 638–642.

173.   As Paul reflects on some of the Old Testament narrative, he says, "These things happened to them as examples and were written down as warnings for us" (1 Corinthians 10:11a).

174.   Defending the authority and reliability of Scripture is critically important but beyond the purposes of this book. For helpful resources, see Craig Blomberg, *Can We Still Believe the Bible? An Evangelical Engagement with Contemporary Questions* (Grand Rapids: Brazos Press, 2014); and Steven Cowen and Terry Wilder, ed. *In Defense of the Bible: A Comprehensive Apologetic for the Authority of Scripture* (Nashville: B&H Academic, 2013).

175.   The preeminence of the *person* of Jesus especially appears in John 5. In an encounter with Jewish leaders, Jesus said, "You study the Scriptures diligently because you think that in them you have eternal life. These are the very Scriptures that testify about me, yet you refuse to come to me to have life" (John 5:39–40). In a sense, they knew a lot about a *book*, but they missed the *person* the book was about!

176.   The Greek word *logos* is employed 331 times in the New Testament with a wide range of meanings. The meanings refer to a word(s), an utterance, a report, a teaching,

reason, etc. See Brown, "Word," in *Dictionary of New Testament Theology*, 3:1106. Revelation says Jesus' "name is the Word of God" (Revelation 19:13b).

177. The term *logos* had a rich philosophical heritage before the time of Jesus. Heraclitus (ca. 500 BC), who thought that everything is in constant flux, also believed the *logos* brought order or stability to the cosmos. The Stoics thought the *logos* structures matter according to its plan. The apostle John may well be incorporating such ideas, but the *logos* for John is not some philosophical principle or cosmic function. The *logos* is God who *came to us* in the *person* of Jesus. For some philosophical background, see John Frame, *A History of Western Philosophy and Theology* (Phillipsburg, NJ: P&R Publishing, 2015), 54–56, 77–78.

178. This is reminiscent of Jesus' conversation with Philip when Philip said, "Lord, show us the Father and that will be enough for us"—to which Jesus replied, "Don't you know me, Philip, even after I have been among you such a long time? Anyone who has seen me has seen the Father. How can you say, 'Show us the Father'?" (John 14:8–9).

179. The Greek word translated as "made him known" (John 1:18) is from *exegeomai*, from which we get the English word "exegesis." The Greek word means to offer an explanation or an interpretation. In a sense, Jesus, as the *logos,* is the *exegesis* of God. The Greek word is "a technical term in Judaism for making known interpretations of the law . . . *and* a term in Greek religion for making known divine truths. The incarnate Word brings from the heart of God a revelation both for Jew and for Greek." A. C. Thiselton, "Explain," in *Dictionary of New Testament Theology*, 1:575.

180. Louw and Nida, *Greek-English Lexicon of the New Testament: Based on Semantic Domains* (New York: United Bible Societies, 1996), 591.

181. Jesus' disciples wanted to know if the man was born blind because of his sin or his parents' sin (John 9:2). The Pharisees accused Jesus of not being from God because he violated the Sabbath, and they denounced both Jesus and the healed man for being sinners (John 9:13–16, 24, 34).

182. Paul claims this new life is a consequence of our baptism. We were "buried with him [Christ Jesus] through baptism into death in order that, just as Christ was raised from the dead through the glory of the Father, we too may live a *new life*" (Romans 6:4).

183. Other notable NIV passages about being "in Christ" include the following (with emphasis given): God is thanked "because of his grace given you *in Christ* Jesus" (1 Corinthians 1:4). "For no matter how many promises God has made, they are 'Yes' *in Christ*" (2 Corinthians 1:20a). "So *in Christ* Jesus you are all children of God through faith" (Galatians 3:26). God "has blessed us in the heavenly realms with every spiritual blessing *in Christ*" (Ephesians 1:3). God's great love "made us alive with Christ . . . and God raised us up with Christ and seated us with him in the heavenly realms *in Christ* Jesus" (Ephesians 2:5a–6). "The dead *in Christ* will rise first" (1 Thessalonians 4:16).

184. Sometimes, the presence of the Holy Spirit produced miraculous signs (e.g., Acts 4:29–31; 10:44–47; cf. 11:15–17; 13:9–11; 19:6) or special visible spiritual gifts (1 Corinthians 12:1–11; 14:1–19). But the "gift of the Holy Spirit" referred to here is a miraculous *indwelling presence*.

185. The Greek word for "sealed" is a past-tense verb (from *sphragizō*). The same word is used to say the tomb of

Jesus was made secure by the Roman guard and had a "seal" placed on the stone in front of it (see Matthew 27:66).

186. The Greek word is the noun *arrabōn*, which the NIV translates as a "deposit guaranteeing." The NASB translates it as "first installment." *Arrabōn* is an ancient business term that involves making a deposit on a debt or putting "earnest money" down for a legal contract. See Johannes Behm, "*Arrabōn*," in *Theological Dictionary of the New Testament,* ed. Gerhard Kittel, Geoffrey W. Bromiley, and Gerhard Friedrich (Grand Rapids: Eerdmans, 1964–), 1:475. The word is used only three times in the New Testament, and each time it refers to the Holy Spirit (Ephesians 1:14; 2 Corinthians 1:22; 5:5).

187. "Abba" is an Aramaic word that means "Father," and it denotes warm intimacy. It was never used in ancient Jewish devotional literature to address God because of the perceived great gap between God and humans. O. Hofius, "Father," in *The New International Dictionary of New Testament Theology*, 1:614. The great gap between God and humans is also stressed in Islam. The notions of God coming in flesh or God's indwelling us with his Spirit are impossible according to the Qur'an. See Winfried Corduan, "A View from the Middle East," in James Sire, *The Universe Next Door*, 249–250.

188. Packer, *Knowing God*, 18.

Made in the USA
Monee, IL
04 September 2021

77379010R00100